Angels on Earth

Past Life
& Spirit World Regressions

Shannon Peck

Angels on Earth

Past Life & Spirit World Regressions

First Edition, Copyright © 2020 by Shannon Peck

Update 2

Lifepath Publishing

1127 Santa Luisa, Solana Beach, CA 92075

All rights reserved. Printed in the United States of America. No part of this book may be reproduced or transmitted in any form or by any means, electronic or mechanical, including photocopying, recording, or by any information storage and retrieval system without written permission from the author, except for the inclusion of quotations in a review.

Cover art by Daniel Holeman: AwakenVisions.com

Cover by Killer Covers

Printed by Amazon Kindle Print

ISBN-13: 9798683211905

Disclaimer: The information contained in this book is not intended as medical advice. The author, publisher, and distributor do not assume responsibility for any adverse consequences resulting from adopting the ideas in this book. It is the hope of the author that, one day, we will no longer need to disclaim information vital to our health, healing, and spiritual progress.

Also by Shannon Peck

Past Life & Spirit World Regressions
Healing Through Revealing Soul

Love Heals
How to Heal Everything with Love

Soul Mate Love
Inside Secrets from an Authentic Soul Mate Couple
Co-authored with Scott Peck

The Love You Deserve
A Spiritual Guide to Genuine Love
Co-authored with Scott Peck

Love Skills You Were Never Taught
Secrets of a Love Master
Co-authored with Scott Peck

Liberating Your Magnificence
Opening Your Life to Infinite Possibilities
Co-authored with Scott Peck

Contents

Books by Shannon Peck

Contents

Introduction ... 7

Part I

Chapter 1: Angels on Earth ... 13

Chapter 2: Spirit Guides, Master Guides, & Archangels ... 21

Chapter 3: How to Listen to Your Guide ... 41

Part II – Past Life Regression Stories

Chapter 4: Cliff – An Interstellar Pilot & Archangel ... 53

Chapter 5: Michelle – A Priestess & Goddess of Light & Divinity ... 71

Chapter 6: Heidi – An Angel of Joy & Creator of Love Explosions ... 91

Chapter 7: Larry – An Angel Clearing Regret, Guilt, & Deep Trauma ... 111

Chapter 8: Wendy – An Angel Healed of Past life Trauma ... 121

Chapter 9: Claire – Even Angels Need Self Protection ... 137

Chapter 10: Jenny – An Angel of Freedom ... 153

Chapter 11: Joanna – An Inter-Galactic Being from an Angelic Realm ... 163

Chapter 12: Petrus – An Angelic Heart of Gold Confronts Ancient Oppression ... 181

Chapter 13: My Own First Regression - Meeting Mother Mary ... 199

About the Author

How to Contact or Book a Session

Introduction

When you think of angels, perhaps images appear in your imagination of Renaissance angels, Tarot cards, angel card decks, or even Biblical angels.

These energies are universal and archetypal and, though many stories refer to their Biblical forms, they are transcendent of all religions.

The angels I write about in this book are souls of the Angelic Realm who live on Earth as humans. They have incarnated in order to help others as well as gain their own lessons.

Following my first regression book, *Past life and Spirit World Regressions, Healing Through Revealing Soul*, I decided to begin writing a second book. That's when my first client from the Angelic Realm arrived. Then, much to my surprise, every single client thereafter, was also from the Angelic Realm.

Once I had sufficient regression stories, my subsequent clients were no longer from the Angelic Realm. I am aware that it is Spirit Guides who bring my clients and me together. It was as though the Spirit Guides decided that this book needed to be written and they sent, one by one, each of their hand-selected souls to my doorstep.

I am intrigued by this phenomenon.

Little did I know that my new book on regression would be about angels on Earth! I give Spirit Guides full credit for the people sent to me and for my clients for their gracious permission to use their regression stories in order to show you what is possible. (In order to remain anonymous, I have given participants a different name.)

I feel honored to have been the regressionist in each of these stories and to work with these highly evolved souls. As I regressed each one, I was aware that I was in a rare position to be able to witness their past lives and the revealing of themselves as truly advanced souls and what that looks like for us all. I think you will find this as intriguing a subject as I have.

As a result of receiving over 55 personal regressions myself and giving hundreds of regressions to others, I'm in an ever-evolving process of spiritual awakening. This work has increased my intuition, showed me how to channel some of the Spirit Guides, and dramatically expanded my spiritual awareness and understanding. These experiences have enabled me to bring all of this spiritual information to you.

I believe that you will benefit just by reading the Spirit World Regression stories. They were received from a deep place of consciousness that we don't normally access. Reading from this place should allow you to recall some of your own past lives or insights into yourself as a soul. These are areas of spirituality rarely discussed on the planet right now, yet they open wide the door to infinite possibilities for us all.

The subjects of Past Life and Spirit World Regression are truly vast. When I write about the Angelic Realm, Master Guides, and Spirit World, please understand that this is an ever-unfolding world to me and it's not the last word by any means.

As a result of giving regressions, I'm always gaining new realizations. Some of these realizations are captured in this book about angels on Earth.

No doubt, if and when I write another book, there will be new discoveries that will have expanded my understanding of the spiritual realm. I have found that new awarenesses do not alter the old ones. Instead, it adds even greater insight, sometimes putting former insights into a new context.

My main purpose as a regressionist is to help my clients reach their Spirit Guide and for them to make a strong connection so that, for the rest of their lives, they will turn to their Spirit Guide for all their needs - receiving comfort, peace, understanding, healing, guidance, and endless other wonderful help as much as they want. In that way, they will lead the strongest, happiest, most empowered lives possible with purpose and spiritual progress. This is my greatest wish for you as well!

Past Life and Spirit World Regressions – the difference

During a Past Life Regression you first visit a past life, then your last day in that life. From there you cross over and go to Spirit World where you meet your Spirit Guide. Your Guide then shows you how the past life relates to your life today. The guide will also assist you to understand your purpose in this life. This is usually where a Past Life Regression ends.

A Spirit World Regression includes all that is in a Past Life Regression and it then continues for about another hour or more where you are in the spiritual realm interacting with your spiritual guides. This is an astounding experience, unlike any other.

About this book

The fact that you are reading this book is evidence of your advanced level as an evolving soul on a spiritual path.

This is a book you can read over and over. Each unique regression will open your insight and deepen your spiritual understanding of what's possible for you.

Every story comes from an actual Spirit World Regression of unparalleled quality - both extraordinary and exceptional, young and old, as you will see.

As you read, you will find yourself exploring new realities which will also bring up new questions and insights about your identity as a soul being and your eternal life journey. This curiosity, when guided, as it is in this book, will evolve you.

PART 1

Chapter 1

Angels on Earth

The Angelic Realm is teeming with angels!

This is a realm where an Earth angel returns when departing from each of their lifetimes. It's where they go in between their lives on Earth or perhaps in between their lives on another star system or galaxy.

Regardless of where they visit on their lifetime journeys, they remain angels through and through. When incarnating on Earth, I refer to them as Earth angels.

Earth angels are, without a doubt, characterized by their sweet, innocent, pure hearts of love, care, and kindness. Their motives are driven by compassion, which enables their life purpose to make things better for all. In the human realm, this doesn't mean Earth angels are perfect, nor does it mean they are *always* loving.

Even from childhood, you can see that their major drive is one of caring for others, driven by a kind heart, being interested in and empathetic towards others. For the most part, they live in consideration of other's feelings and well-being.

However, they have their moments of stress, confusion, doubts, emotional overload, and suffering, along with having personal needs for peace and freedom from Earth problems.

Once they enter Earth life, they become like all humans, often forgetting their divine origin, taking on human problems, experiencing emotions, along with trauma, loss, grief, anger, and all the varied things other humans experience. The difference is that they bring their angelic quality of love into everything.

Earth angels are often people's chosen best friends because people sense their love and being able to count on them for understanding, respect, trustworthiness, consideration, listening, forgiveness, good heartedness, kindness, and patience. Angels are also great celebrators of anything positive.

How Earth angels become spiritually evolved

Some angels have evolved for far longer periods than others. This generally means they carry more wisdom from having faced and successfully addressed many difficult and complex problems. Their mistakes will vary depending on their evolution. Just as everyone on Earth, they too are here to learn lessons and gain wisdom. But, no matter how evolved they are, the thing that most stands out for these souls is their lovingkindness.

The Angelic Realm is always with you

Being of the divine realm, heavenly angels are infinite in number. While not all angels incarnate, others are just beginning their Angelic Realm evolution. During especially difficult times on Earth, more souls from the Angelic Realm may be sent to offer their special help.

The Angelic Realm is always with you. This is true whether or not you are from the Angelic Realm. This realm is a gift for us all.

The Angelic Realm is felt as a magnificent presence. You can call on angels anytime and they will help you. They tend to feel more plural than singular, acting in unity rather than as individual angels. Here are a few ways you may experience or sense them as they:

- Hover over you
- Gather around you
- Surround you
- Encircle you
- Penetrate you with their loving, healing energies
- Cause you to feel their presence
- Cause you to feel comfort, peace, worthiness, love, and calm
- Offer you divine guidance

Sometimes when you feel their presence, you may experience goose bumps or a chill down your spine. You may have noticed other ways they have of letting you know when they are with you, such as through your intuition, which increases with use.

Are you an Earth angel?

As you read about Earth angel characteristics below, you may consider which of these you most recognize in yourself and perhaps other people you know or have known. This will also help you to see if you are of the Angelic Realm.

Whether you are from the Angelic Realm or not, please know that, because of your divine origin, you play an equally important role on Earth. You are equally worthy and deserving of all good, including all love.

Being heart-based, Earth Angels do a world of things for you. They may do many of the following things:

- Offer loving support and kind help
- Draw from their wisdom and intelligence for you
- Empower you
- Offer you their healing presence
- Empathize
- Understand
- Listen
- Bless
- Provide generosity from their heart which often spills into good acts for you
- Help to orchestrate good things to benefit you
- Stand tall with you while offering their support so you feel their strength
- Connect you to the Angelic Realm
- Stand with you in faith, hope, and joy to help you weather a storm

Their presence often:

- Calms
- Inspires
- Soothes
- Comforts
- Guards
- Encourages
- Strengthens
- Lifts
- Assures

- Causes you to feel loved.

What angels generally do not do:
- Gossip
- Criticize destructively
- Complain a lot
- Hold a grudge
- Seek revenge (at least not for long, as they'd rather let things go)
- Hate (at least not for long - they seek calm and to stay with love)
- Shame, demean, or bully another
- Judge you when a deeper understanding and compassion are needed (however, they know to discern when wrong is being done)
- Harm another intentionally
- Lack a conscience after doing something they regret

Their main problems on Earth

The main problem of Earth angels is over giving or over sacrificing and even martyrdom, to the point of almost making themselves non-existent, lost as a result of their generosity and unselfishness. Because they are loving, they can be misunderstood to be weak. These are generally among their biggest lessons.

Angels have a need to be accountable for their energy and where it is given so it isn't overused by themselves in giving to others, thereby distracting and draining them where they get off course of being able to give their gifts where most needed. This is true for all souls as well. Angels tend to put others first, above their own needs. This can produce the problem of a major imbalance.

They get perplexed by peoples' inhumanity to people, animals, and the environment. Injustices, acts of violence, and selfish behaviors such as greed, inequities, and harming others trouble them greatly. Their sensitivity only grows larger with their evolution.

While love comes easily to them, the wisdom of self-protection does not. They can be unaware of others who take advantage of them.

Being quick to forgive and forget unfairness and injustice towards themselves can cause Earth angels to become enablers. In this role, some angels can become easy prey to controlling, dominating people who are attracted to Earth angels for being a mate or a best friend. Earth angels can become mortally wounded from this.

Being extremely giving and wanting to help when you are in need, their tendency is to focus on others more than themselves. Although they come to Earth with the Angelic Realm accompanying them, they often forget and believe they are all alone and they carry great burdens for others, making sacrifices and extending big efforts to offer support, love, and healing. This is often where their energy goes.

It may take lifetimes for Earth angels to find their own voice, give equal consideration to themselves as they do for others, and learn to speak up for themselves in a loving, effective way without backing down. All of these angelic qualities are derived from their two most Iconic Archangels – Michael and Mother Mary, who are endowed with divine Love, spiritual healing, and powerful divine strength, courage, and protection.

What Earth angels most need is to stand tall in their love, find their voice and learn to speak up and be strong, and give equal consideration to themselves as they do to others. It can be challenging for them to learn to set boundaries and hold their value in high esteem, while being wise to reserve their energies for their angelic work on Earth and for those who truly need them. In this way, they can pour out their energies of love as angels do so well. This may take many, many lifetimes.

For most people, their evolution centers around becoming more loving. And, certainly for us all, this is a point of our highest evolution. However, with angels, their ease of loving has a great advantage to their evolution. Once they awaken to their angelic power, there's no stopping them.

What it's like for angels on Earth

All souls who incarnate on Earth are here to learn lessons and grow in wisdom. We all come from a place that is divine, created by Love itself. Everyone on Earth shares these things in common.

In every regression story in this book, my client learned, for the first time, about being from the Angelic Realm during their regression with me. At first, they were surprised but then began to recognize their true self in this higher context. When they left the regression session, they often told me that they still felt the presence of the Angelic Realm accompanying them.

This presence comes in many ways as I discuss in the next chapter.

Chapter 2

Spirit Guides, Master Guides, & Archangels

There are many reasons people arrive at my door for a Past Life Regression.

We often meet our Spirit Guides and Master Guides in Spirit World when having a Past Life or Spirit World Regression. This is one of the greatest moments in these regressions.

This is usually the first time that someone becomes fully aware of having a spiritual guide. Once they meet their guide and interact, my clients often tell me that they recalled times in their lives when their guide came to them and was present with them – especially at a difficult time. It's an awakening moment. They tend to be both shocked and grateful to learn the news of having a guide.

Guides are spiritually advanced and that is why they are in a guide role. I use the words power, love, and holiness to begin their description.

Here's what I've learned about Spirit Guides, followed by what I've learned about Master Guides.

Spirit Guides

A Spirit Guide is a soul that has awakened and matured sufficiently in Spirit where they can be capable of guiding other souls. This is a very advanced being. As a guide, they bring great wisdom, love, and intelligence to whoever they are guiding.

You may find your Spirit Guide appear in a form that surprises you. Spirit Guides often appear as a male, a female, a grandmother, a face, a wizard, a light, a holy presence, or even an animal figure. Sometimes multiple Spirit Guides appear together.

I tell you this because some clients have not understood that their Spirit Guide may appear in a variety of ways and they may shun the form in which their Spirit Guide appears, preferring perhaps something more spiritual and beautiful.

If you can get past the form, you can recognize and appreciate that your guide is a highly advanced being who knows you intimately. Your guide is intently interested in your well-being and is even looking after you in powerful ways to help you stay on course of your life purpose and to prevent you from making major mistakes that could ruin your life.

A Spirit Guide may be with you short term or long term – over lifetimes - depending on what your soul is learning and needing and how long it takes you to learn the particular lessons.

It's extremely valuable to your life and well-being to live in close connection with your Spirit Guide. This is one of the major beings who is helping you develop spiritually – with your soul, your lessons - and to watch over you and respond whenever you call. Whether or not you call on them, they are always with you and instantly available to you.

Master Guides

A Master Guide is different from a Spirit Guide. I sense that they are the ones who are behind the Spirit Guide and leading them.

Master Guides are of an extremely high calibration of energy, power, love, guidance, action, intelligence, capability, and strength! I sense that a Master Guide is an ascended soul of great spiritual magnitude, power, and love.

During a regression, at the point when a guide appears, your Spirit Guide may fade or disappear, allowing your Master Guide to lead.

When we pray for guidance, any one of these Master Guides can be instantly listening and responding. In a Spirit World Regression, you quickly realize the immortal loving care and wise oversight you have received all your life from your celestial hosts!

When a Master Guide appears during a regression, it's usually an impressive event. Often my client will have some tears or even cry, so deeply touched and overwhelmed by their Master Guide's love and power.

Master Guides sometime appear as a small light and then a few minutes later, as you become more acclimated to them, you soon feel enveloped by a light that's so bright it surpasses the sun, yet you can still easily look at them.

When I've asked a Master Guide how long they have been with my client, the answer has always been "forever."

I sense that a Master Guide is an ascended soul of great spiritual magnitude, power, and love. I almost feel like I'm in the presence of God when one or more of them appear. You generally have one Master Guide who leads you. However, during a regression, there could be others who appear as well.

Sometimes, after a client has met their Master Guide, I ask my client to imagine a mirror in front of them and to describe their own image. My clients often report that they look like their Master Guide.

It's usually somewhat startling but there is a feeling of belonging with the Master Guide as well. This is one of the most interesting times during a regression, where I often ask questions of the Master Guide in order for my client to learn about themselves as a soul. This can be a life-changing event.

With a Master Guide, there is a sense of belonging and care. The relationship is indescribably beautiful.

Being in the presence of your Master Guide is so significant that you can, perhaps for the first time, view yourself as a soul. This begins to answer the question, "Who am I?"

As a result, many new spiritual understandings come into view. It advances you spiritually whenever you are in the presence of your guide because this encounter awakens you to the fact you are a soul and that you actually have a Spirit Guide. This is a paradigm shift for most. Each time this experience occurs can set you on a course of coming into an even greater spiritual awakening.

Once you meet your Spirit Guide or Master Guide, you gain a new awareness, and your spirituality becomes more alive as you realize you can engage with your guide at any time and as often as you wish. You realize you are never alone.

Seeing your immortality enables you to come to terms with your soul as well as your life problems living as a human. It offers a very different and enlarged perspective of yourself and gives you a context to see your purpose and place in all things. It also enables you to begin addressing inner truths about your true self. Your spiritual insight expands.

With our guides, we feel known, recognized, understood, empowered, and loved. It's amazing to the depth at which you can feel this and how much it means.

Meetings with your guide give a tremendous spiritual boost, offering insights that not only advance your soul or Higher Self, but also often provide clearings from blocks as well as healing and specific guidance for where you are at that moment in your life.

Your guide's help is immense and it is help that you cannot create for yourself nor gain through any other source.

Once you meet or come to know your guide, you can sense their presence when they are with you. And you can sense your own light increasing and becoming more like your guide's.

I've come to realize that we are all made of light – which has a frequency, vibration, and color. As we learn and grow over endless lifetimes, our light brightens and enlarges as we develop on our individual soul journeys. I believe that our light represents our awakened divinity. There's an evolutionary process at work within each of our souls.

Our guides are tremendously helpful to our evolutionary process of enlightening as we learn to call on them on a regular basis – for everything. Consider that the more you call on them, the more you will become like them. This is the highest spiritual training of all. And it's available to everyone equally.

My understanding of the Master Guides came through regressions where I met each one. Even now, new ones often present themselves.

Clients who are from the Angelic Realm are usually guided by one of the Master Guides as you will see in this book. I think of the Master Guides as divine beings or energies. They are part of the divine Allness from which we are all derived.

Archangel Michael is a Master Guide and the Patriarch of the Angelic Realm

Archangel Michael is the Patriarch of the Angelic Realm. His presence is omnipotent and magnificent with love.

At times, during a regression, Michael may present himself as a soft white light. Other times, his soft white light may expand to reveal his powerful radiance as an extremely bright White Light that exudes pure love.

Archangel Michael is the lead angel with an absolute, incalculable divine authority and boldness. He doesn't always reveal his full power, but when he does, it's almost shocking. And his love is equally felt.

I think of him as the Angel Patriarch and Protector.

In regressions, he is able to communicate his messages by causing the person to know, sense, or feel something that is penetratingly true. One thing is for sure. You won't soon forget him. From the moment you meet him, you will always want to be with him. And you may discover when you reach out to him, he is already there with you.

As Lord Protector, he's in full charge of the Angelic Realm.

Mary, Mother of Love – a Master Guide

Mary, Mother of Love, is the Grand Matriarch of the Angelic realm. She presents the feminine equivalent of divine Love. Like Michael, her love is divine and all-powerful. She's sometimes referred to as Mary, an ascended master, or Mother Mary.

When Mary appears, you feel an immediate immersion of love.

During a personal regression, Mother Mary revealed her entire band of angels to me. The angels looked like an illuminated band of sparkling white lights, glistening.

Once, on a sunny day I paused to looked at the Pacific Ocean, which caught my attention. As the waves crested with the sun shining on the waters, it reminded me of what I saw as Mary's band of angels in my regression. The sparkling lights were indistinguishable from each other and looked like a mass of moving, clear, luminescent lights. They were almost identical to Mary's band of angels shown to me.

Quan Yin sometimes appears with Mother Mary. They both represent divine Love and infinite compassion characterizing a Master Guide.

Mother Mary and Archangel Michael – Matriarch and Patriarch of Angels

You can express Mary's divine Mothering qualities whether or not you are a mother. Even children have nurturing, caring, loving qualities of Mother Mary. Motherhood is one aspect of Mary. Healing with unconditional divine Love is another. Whether Mary is mothering or healing, she's an unequalled powerhouse of love. So are you!

Mary lives within the heart of many mothers and women who truly have the pure mothering gifts of caring, nurturing, protective love. She operates to bring healing through a mother's love. Men or fathers also have this mother love quality.

You may have noticed that I refer to Mary as an archangel in the Angelic Realm while also acknowledging that she has her own band of angels. She's everywhere that love is.

You can express Archangel Michael's fathering qualities whether nor not you are a father. As a powerfully strong protector, he carries absolute divine authority in the purest sense. So can you!

When we think of human authority, we often think of the ego's desire to control and dominate, often using tactics of physical force or emotional shaming and demoralizing. However, these are not divine qualities and are the opposite of Archangel Michael's power, which is one of omnipotent, pure love, and partnership.

Michael lives within the hearts of many fathers, men, women, and children who have the gifts and mission of love and protection.

Golden Light – a Master Guide

Golden Light is a Master Guide of immense intelligence, power, wisdom, and love. It's spectacular.

It has a way of communicating with few words, however, the meaning is clearly received by you.

Golden Light emits its light as a powerful presence. Its light not only shines and radiates, it also permeates and envelops. I often hear clients describe, when they first meet Golden Light, that its Light is, first in front of them, then it is permeating and enveloping them. Often it becomes vastly enormous in size, all-encompassing and unending.

It's light and power seem to be without limit.

Golden Light is a unifier and it is, within itself, completely unified. Being indivisible, it's impossible to separate it into parts. It represents our divine wholeness and well-being.

As a Master Guide, Golden Light is everywhere and can manifest through its qualities of love as it envelops, permeates, and unifies. It's miraculous to see Golden Light manifest on Earth through people. My husband, a rarified being, is a great example.

During a regression, sometimes many Master Guides show up such as occurred in Heidi's Spirit World Regression. However, usually only one Master Guide will be in the lead for your regression.

Other archangel guides who appear in this book

Archangels are impressive and powerful. However, outside of archangel Michael, I am not completely sure that other archangels are Master Guides as archangel Michael and Mother Mary.

Since these additional archangels are of the Angelic Realm, I'll mention a few who have come through regressions:

- Archangel Chamuel, acted as a protector in Claire's regression.
- Archangel Youlot came from another universe and appeared in Cliff's regression, who was also an archangel. (He was so much fun!)
- Archangel Gabriella appeared in Michelle's regression.
- Archangels Gabriel, Arielle, and Uriel appeared in Heid's regression. Gabriel also appeared in Wendy's regression.

I am always surprised and delighted to continue learning about the many archangels.

Master guidance from Collectives

A Collective often appears once my client has arrived in Spirit World after dying from their past life.

At first, I notice my client is sharing with me what their Spirit Guide or Master Guide or Council of Elders is saying to them. As time goes on during the regression, my client speaks *as* the Collective group of those divine beings who have gathered to interact with my client.

My client may use the pronoun "I," but when I ask who is speaking, my client will say it's everyone. There is no longer an individuation between my client and the group. They are speaking as one. At times, my client may have difficulty going back and forth conveying to me what is being told by the group since the pattern of telepathy is rapid and voluminous.

I consider this Master guidance and for this reason I mention it here.

There are 2 other types of Collectives which I do not consider to be equivalent to Master guidance. They gather for a different reason and function differently.

Your Soul Family Collective

A Soul Family is the group of souls you return to after your Earth life. A Soul Family often agrees to incarnate at the same time, playing different roles with each other on Earth in order to help each other grow and learn lessons, developing opportunities to improve each other's' karma.

Members of your Soul Family may appear in your current life as a member of your family, a spouse, or a close friend. They sometimes take on an adversarial role that you two have agreed upon in advance in order to help you learn an important karmic lesson, which you signed up for. However, please do not assume that someone who is abusive to you is there because you have a soul agreement with them or that you need this person for karmic reasons.

In Spirit World, in between your lives, you often return immediately to your Soul Family to learn and study together in order to make plans and evolve to higher frequencies. You are bonded through love and purpose. It's always a happy homecoming when you exit Earth to return to your Soul Family in Spirit World.

Sometimes, just one representative of an entire Soul Family may decide to incarnate on Earth in human form. This individual acts as an emissary to the Soul Family group, or Collective. During its time on Earth, the emissary – which may be you - remains connected to its Soul Family, in order for its entire group to be able to experience Earth life through their emissary.

Angelic Realm Collective

Another Collective relates to the Angelic Realm. Whenever Earth angels incarnate, they always have their Angelic Realm of angels with them and can call on them for help, along with their archangel or their Spirit Guide, usually of the Angelic Ream as well. As such, they operate as a Collective. Their purpose for remaining connected, however, is not so those of the Angelic Realm can experience life on Earth through a representative.

The Angelic Realm remains connected to its Earth angels in order to offer its continual support which is available for help, love, protection and guidance at all times. During a Spirit World Regression, I am nearly always aware of a fluttering of divine angels accompanying my client.

The good news is that the Angelic Realm is always available to you as well. You can call on your angels for help anytime. They want you to do this and often. No matter is too small. No call is too soon since the last time you called on them. That's how much they love and care for you. This is their mission and what they do best. In this way, they contribute to the whole of us all as One.

Jesus – a Master Guide

Jesus has appeared wearing a deep blue robe, emanating love, compassion, and forgiveness. He's been described wearing a beard and smiling, penetrating you with pure love while gazing into your eyes. It's as though, by his very presence, all your wrongs are absolved and fall away. At times, he appears standing with outstretched arms welcoming you with open love, which has almost overwhelmed some of my clients.

In Heidi's regression, he appeared with great humor, making us laugh out loud. Heidi is an Earth angel comedian who really brought out Jesus' playful nature as he whisked her up in his chariot and they zoomed off together to her Council of Elders meeting – with Jesus at the helm! During the ride, angels darted in and out of the chariot windows, laughing playfully as they travelled rapidly. Upon arrival, Jesus almost crash landed the chariot, but did it in a funny way as though it was a plane coming in entirely too fast.

Although he proved himself comedic, showing a playful, fun side, while purposefully delivering my client to her Council, he's usually more quiet and still, as a holy divine presence and true Master Guide.

At times, Jesus appears as one of several Master Guides where one takes a lead. It's a spectacular experience to have multiple Master Guides present during a Spirit World Regression.

Radiant, intense colors of some of the Master Guides

Master Guides are often recognized by their radiant color and their powerful effects, which carry extremely high vibrations.

I'll share 5 Master Guides and their radiant colors which have been seen – and experienced – by myself and many of my clients during a Spirit World Regression.

Archangel Michael's powerful strength, love, and protection are emitted through his pure, white light.

Mary, Mother Love, is mostly radiant gold and blue. There's a bright golden light coming from her heart chakra, representing her spiritual healing power, which is unlimited. This golden light is surrounded by an intense, vibrant blue light radiating her divine, infinite love outwards into the universe. Her enormous nurturing, healing love is emitted through her light.

Golden Light is bright gold, brighter than the sun but without making you squint. It's gigantic Light of Guidance encompasses, envelops, and unites.

These colors carry very high frequencies from the divine realm.

In my experience, the Collective is usually invisible. Rather than appearing as a visual color of light, it is sensed more as a divine presence, a gathering of many who are acting as one. Its presence is felt in a powerful way. Whether visible or invisible, the Collective is truly profound.

Jesus often appears as a hazy full-bodied form or face which is recognized by a profound love and knowingness. I'm told by clients that when he looks at you, he has a deeply personal and loving smile as though he knows you intently.

At times, Jesus and Mary, individually, have been described wearing a robe of deep blue.

Through their presence as light, Master Guides help us understand divine Spirit's unimaginable power and love, which is incomprehensible and yet it is in all things and people, including yourself.

Each Master Guide offers continual spiritual help, comfort, love, healing, and guidance. Whenever we ask for it, we are given massive influxes of their powerful, loving help. They are always present and responsive when we ask for them.

Since we are all of a divine source, we are capable of taking on some of the high qualities of Master Guides. The plan is for us to stay close to our guides and grow in spiritual pureness as we also learn to bring our spirituality into our motives and actions on Earth and to our relationships. All of us are capable of so much more spiritual love, power, presencing, beauty, divinity, and healing.

Though I cannot imagine what it must be like to be an ascended master, I believe that we are each on a path of ascension. Through learning lessons and advancing in awareness and wisdom, we evolve. Our path is one of light and eternity.

The Council of Elders

People who have a Spirit Word Regression are often led by their guides to visit their Council of Elders, who are highly evolved beings full of love and wisdom for you. They help to bring enormous clarity to who you are and your life purpose. Much like Master Guides, they are highly involved with your soul, overseeing its eternal progress and well-being.

They watch over you and help you, always hoping you will connect with them so that you will be able to avoid making important mistakes. You meet them during the longer Spirit World Regression.

Through the Council of Elders, - and also through your Spirit Guides - you gain tremendous insights into yourself as an immortal soul, your overall purpose, the path you've been on throughout lifetimes, and how well you are doing.

The interaction is amazing because you are not only visiting them as a soul, but they are spiritual beings who know your soul and are capable of imparting guidance from a very high level of knowledge and all-seeing. They can also address your present problems, answer questions, offer healing, and give you an experience of empowerment, comfort, and confidence. It's truly an awakening experience.

A client's Master Guide sometimes accompanies them during this visit to the Council of Elders.

Often, however, with the appearance of a Master Guide, there may be no need to visit the Council of Elders. And sometimes, as in the case with archangel Michael, he may be the head of your Council of Elders, which may turn out to be a Council of Angels.

Highly evolved individuals may find themselves as a member of their Council of Elders, or even one of its lead members.

Archangels' wings

Whenever Michael's wings are fully open, my clients are in awe. His wings have appeared in different sizes and proportions. Sometimes his wings are cosmic in size. At other times, they appear elaborately large.

With his wings open, it represents a show of power, joy, and celestial being.

However, he can accomplish everything with his wings in any position, whether fully open, unopened, or mid-open - also whether he reveals them partially or at their full length.

Curious about their wings, I've wondered about their purpose. As a result, I've come to believe 3 reasons they open their wings.

- Wings can open to show a pronouncement of power or authority.
- Half open wings, such as Archangel Gabriella's, indicated her state of happiness, lovingness, and warmth. (This is in Michelle's regression in this book.)
- Wings may also open in response to an archangel's sense of elation, celebration, or expression of pure joy. These high vibrations are not human emotions. They are more like a celestial hallelujah!

I'll share with you a description of archangel Michael's wings that one of my clients gave me when she interacted with him in her regression. This is covered more fully in my book, *Past Life & Spirit World Regressions, Healing Through Revealing Soul*.

She described him as a magnificent large, white robed angel. He was sitting on a big, white horse overlooking a high cliff. His wings were large and prominent, and he was positioned in the middle of a row of other angelic riders all overlooking the same cliff.

Michael then dismounted from his horse and he did something that my client and I will never forget. Standing behind her, he removed his enormous white wings and placed them over her shoulders for her to experience and wear!

In fact, I recall that his wings were as sleeves that he put on her as one would assist putting on another's coat. As she wore Michael's wings she also became aware that his wings began from her shoulders and went all the way to the ground. We were in awe!

Regardless of whether Archangel Michael is standing or sitting, the love that pours out of him can be felt in every bone of your body.

Channeling for the Master Guides

When I first channeled for Golden Light, it was during a Spirit World Regression. As I asked my client's questions, Golden Light answered indirectly and vaguely in a teasing way, making jokes and suggesting that I knew the answer to the questions, telling my client, "Ask Shannon."

I couldn't imagine why. I felt quite sure that I couldn't do it accurately. However, once I began, Golden Light verified I did it right and it had a way of encouraging me to do more of it, as though It wanted me at the helm.

Often, when Golden Light enters my husband's regressions, its humor is prominent, even showing a casualness about answering my questions, perhaps amused. But also its humor is used to calm my intense passion wanting to know and understand all things spiritual. I laugh too! I feel humbled to be involved in any way.

At times, though not often, when my client is blocked and can't access their guide, I sense the message that the Master Guide wants to convey. The message comes to me as my own thought. With an intuitive sense of understanding about what is taking place in the regression, I am able to put it together and bring overall clarity. These clients have been relieved and gratified feeling my help was useful. When I ask my client to check with their guide to see if I channeled accurately, they say that I did.

Master Guides have a surprising sense of humor. During some moments, my client and I find ourselves laughing, even uproariously. Some regressions can be great fun!

Whenever I do spiritual healing work, I channel Mother Mary. I did this for many years without knowing where the inspiring and powerful information was coming from before I met her - except that I knew it was divinely sourced. Then, when I met Mary, I knew.

You, too, may discover yourself channeling for the Master Guides as you ask them for help to utilize your spiritual intuition in supporting your loved ones, friends, or clients.

Is it possible you just made up your Master Guide? Does it matter?

Many clients wonder if they are just making things up in their regressions – including their spiritual guides.

Being an open-minded metaphysician, it's not a hard stretch for me to think it's possible that your Master Guides are part of your infinite consciousness that you haven't yet tapped into and that hasn't yet come into realization until your regression. Our infinity is unimaginable to us.

Your regressed state brings in information from your Superconscious, which holds memories from all your past lives. Within this Superconscious mind, you have recall of your Master Guides as well, which may just be parts of yourself – your divine, infinite Self - that you think are separate and yet are not. I sometimes think of us as a giant Collective of All That Exists - as one.

Ultimately, I believe we will all come to see that we are not separate but one, and a united, cohesive expression of the Divine – by whatever name you know it by.

During a Spirit World Regression, the reality of your guide becomes self-evident when you interact and learn that your guide knows you deeply and intimately in a caring, loving way – and offers help. As you experience your guide's wisdom, meeting you exactly where you are in this moment of your life, many doubts fall away. This would be hard to make up!

Chapter 3

How to Listen to Your Guide

One of the most valuable things I've learned since I began my spiritual journey, back in the 1970's, is that I'm not alone. I have guides to turn to. So do you. Listening to them is the key to connecting with them.

In staying close to my guides or divine guidance, I've experienced help far beyond my human capacity. You can experience this too. What happens from practicing this over the years is that your connection grows stronger, as does your intuition. And you may find yourself connecting with far more frequency and receive far more help.

For example, during the course of my day, or during the night, I may begin to feel a little disconnected, which may be accompanied by anxiety. Something feels off. That's when I tune in. The sooner I do it, the sooner I feel relief. I've learned that there's often an immediacy about tuning in. Anxiety tends to build.

If I'm with others, I may need to excuse myself and take a brief pause to be alone. If I can't excuse myself, I go ahead and tune in, right there in the midst of a conversation or of whatever is going on around me. It only takes a moment to say, "Please help me." Certainly, for most all of my decisions I ask for divine guidance or check in to sense it.

I also love to start each day by listening for divine guidance. I begin by thinking of my loved ones, including myself, and offering blessings of love, purpose, prosperity, grace, good health, protection, inspiration, focus, joy, and other things that come to mind.

More than a mere rehearsal of steps or words, I feel my heart giving this blessing through my love as it pours over us all. Then, I proceed to bless others including my country and the world and many other things that concern me at the time.

There is no set way you need to learn to ask for help. Whatever you say or think quietly is more than adequate. Whatever comes out first is the right thing. "Help!" or "I need help!" or "I need you!" or "Please!" or "I'm open now."

At that moment, there's nothing more important than making a connection with your guides. This takes precedence over everything else that's occurring. You need to feel stronger, closer, and more connected to the divine, to your own divine or Higher Self, where you feel strong, balanced, capable, and in touch with your heart filled with joy and love.

Your guides already know you need help. In fact, when you feel aware of being disconnected, it's probably your guides who are giving you that prompting to turn to them. They are waiting for you to ask.

One thing I've learned repeatedly while giving Past Life and Spirit World Regressions, is that the guides are trying ever so hard to get our attention - over lifetimes - in order to offer their divine, loving guidance. That's so we will suffer far less. Each time you ask, you'll get help.

Once I'm aware of my need for spiritual help, I tune in. I listen, with my whole heart, until I know I have the connection and am beginning to feel the presence of guidance. It could be instant. It could take longer, but from the time you ask for help, it starts to come in.

At first, I may sense divine help as a subtle presence. The most subtle feeling can bring comfort right away, even though nothing else has happened. It's a sign. Continuing to listen, it comes in stronger.

I sometimes journal, agreeing with myself to write down only what is "coming" to me as a result of asking for help. This focus helps to keep out distracting thoughts that would take me away from listening to something so refined.

It's important to remember that guidance occurs from a simple turning towards the divine for help. Your asking begins the process.

Feeling divine help is wonderful. You're immediately aware that you are being accompanied on your life journey. You feel strength, uplift, and even loving companionship. New truth begins to dawn about your life and how to live it in a better way.

On big issues, I connect strongly and stay tuned in, while aware that by doing so, I'm in my most right place. I can settle in for the day or for days ahead.

On issues that are emotional, with high fear, anxiety, worry, or feeling down, I stick like glue to my guides, listening and being wide open to guidance.

At those times, I may be less likely to be aware of clear, immediate guidance due to the emotion. I may just go for a feeling of closeness as I come into greater calm. Then the guidance comes in clearer.

Once, after some x-rays of my mouth, my dentist explained many complex dental treatments I would be needing including surgery, new crowns, a root canal, and other things. I was overwhelmed by the shock of so many needs as well as imagining the cost. Fighting back tears, I turned to my guide, even as the dentist was still speaking, and I heard, "Courage!" I held to that thought like glue. Within minutes, I felt calmer.

Once the multiple appointments were made addressing my dental needs, I found myself once again in fear and with dread of it all. As I prayed once again about this - and daily - I eventually started to relax and rely on the source I was turning to.

Even during a long appointment with a lot of drilling, I turned to Mother Mary and found myself feeling flooded with her healing love, enabling me to be distracted from the loud and invasive sensation of the drill.

Looking back on that period, I can tell you that my prayers didn't prevent my having to deal with each and every one of the procedures outlined for me. But my prayers had a huge influence on how well each procedure went.

Even while being given shots, I felt the presence of angels and had very little pain. In fact, this was true for all of the procedures. During this time, our income increased sufficient to cover the costs. I was so grateful and felt my guides had taken me through the entire ordeal.

At other times, when I feel uninspired, drained, stressed, or distant from my spiritual connection, I find a moment to sit down, become still, and, after asking for guidance, I'll spend time writing what comes to me. While doing this, it may not seem impressive. But when I read it over, and it sinks in, I'm often astounded how perfect the guidance is. (For more examples of spiritual healings, see *Love Heals, How to Heal Everything with Love*).

We need daily guidance. And we need guidance at every turn, especially now during these turbulent times where it's hard to feel a secure footing. Any and all understanding of my life - my circumstances and how to navigate them - comes from divine guidance and from tuning in, listening and following the guidance as best I can.

No matter what you are presently facing and even though you may not know how you will ever be able to see your way through it, your guides and the entire Angelic Realm always have a wonderful plan for you that is unimaginable to you. Stay close until the light dawns, little by little. And it will.

How you can connect with Master Guides during a regression

A Spirit World Regression is a session where you can connect more deeply with one of the iconic Spirit Guides. Your guide will appear.

Sometimes there may be a different guide that shows up to help you transition from Earth to the Spirit Realm. The transition guide may be brief and provide healing if your past life was traumatic or especially hard.

Once you cross over to Spirit World and have been greeted, I ask your Spirit Guide to come forward. We discover its name and description and then, while you're processing having a Spirit Guide, we proceed to ask questions and have interaction to learn the reason your guide chose that particular past life to show you and to learn how it applies to your life today.

Your guide may want to take you somewhere, such as to your Council of Elders where you can do a deeper review of your life among highly evolved beings who care deeply about you and have known you forever.

This is where a Spirit World Regression becomes most meaningful to you. My goal is to help connect and deepen you with your Council or perhaps a Master Guide so that you will see how powerful their help can be and how wonderful their love is for you and you will want to live closely in touch for the rest of your life.

This, in fact, has been my life devotion – practicing a daily, on-going connection with my guide. It's the biggest blessing I could wish for you.

This moment of connection is the greatest potential transformation of a regression, although there are other immediate powerful moments learning about your soul and it's journey as well.

What it means to stay in connection with your guide after your regression

Living from a continual, open connection to your guide provides a rich life of trust and confidence that you are not acting alone and that you are being divinely guided.

You can call on your guides anytime and ask for guidance. It doesn't matter what time of day or how many times you have addressed the same problem. They are always with you.

I've heard people tell me that they don't want to bother their guide since they already have so much to deal with for others. However, imagine saying to the sun, "I don't want to bother you to shine on me since there are so many others on Earth who need your sunshine." Ask for guidance.

Be sure, after you ask for their help, that you show up and listen.

The spiritual realm can evade us since we have a gazillion distractions that keep us from slowing down sufficiently to tune in and receive guidance and then confirm that we got the help.

It's easy to tell yourself that you asked and then nothing happened - no one showed up and no help was received.

I believe it's impossible not to receive help when we ask the divine realm. We merely need to assume responsibility to become quiet, take a few breaths, calm down, listen.

Make space in your life to receive guidance. For years I found it very helpful when I asked for help to sit quietly with a pen and pad in hand, ready to record any word or message I received, no matter how vague at the time. This was one of the greatest learning experiences of my life and it taught me how to listen for divine guidance, which developed my intuition and continues to do so.

Today, I find it easy and fast to tune in and receive an almost immediate response for my request. It's not because I am so advanced or favored that I get special treatment. It's simply because I have practiced receiving guidance exactly as I have described here and as a result, I have come to understand that the guidance was not only fast, it was instant. And oftentimes, the guidance comes in *as* I ask for it. This is a beautiful way to live.

Your needs are already known by your guides.

What happens in your life when you don't connect with your Guides?

The number one complaint I hear from guides is that we don't listen to them or ask them for help. You can be so much happier if you check in with your guides.

A great spiritual awakening occurs when you realize your need for staying close to your guide and listening for its guidance. It's a mark of significant spiritual growth and is the beginning of empowerment and entering the spiritual realm while still on Earth. I believe that a big part of your life purpose is to bring down Spirit World qualities into your life through your skills of intuition and learning to follow divine guidance. This nurtures your spiritual growth in magnificent ways.

Not checking in with your guide creates great burden and adds unnecessary stress for you. I feel this is the saddest and biggest problem that people have. You don't want to miss out on all that support and help, protection and love.

People tend to live with the illusion that they are here on their own and must do their own spiritual work alone. Nothing could be further from the truth. What a hardship that creates for you!

When you don't reach out to your guides, the entire spiritual realm remains vague, as does much of what you're doing on Earth.

I've learned through regressions that your guides, when contacted, can prevent suffering and big mistakes, even from ruining your life. Just as a child needs and benefits from having wise, loving, caring parents, we too need and benefit from connecting with our Master Guides and on a regular basis. How much love and protection do you want in your life? That's how often you should reach out to them.

Once you get to know your guide, its help can be activated in your life, which will accelerate your spiritual growth and lift you to greater spiritual heights.

The goal is to develop a relationship with your guide and learn to tune in and ask for help and guidance. Life, then, becomes easier and softer, more confident, peaceful and happier. Your guides want this for you. It will also help develop your intuition so that you can live in a constant stream of connection with them. This will empower and transform your entire life to new levels.

The biggest part of my work as a regressionist is to help connect my client to their guide. This is often an essential point of transformation in a regression.

What you are about to read

The following chapters tell the true stories of each individual I regressed who is from an Angelic Realm. By reading these amazing stories, you will find yourself expanding as you gain a great deal of insight and awareness. This may bring up things you recall or know at a very deep level about yourself.

My suggestion is that, if you find yourself stirring within, ask your spiritual guide to help you as you continue to read and ponder. Whether or not you have identified your guide doesn't matter.

I hope that by reading this book you will begin to identify yourself as a soul and the eternal path you have taken, along with the help and comfort that is available to you.

Let the following pages act as your guide to your awakening as a soul. Let's start with Cliff, an interstellar pilot who is also an archangel from another realm.

PART 2

Spirit World Regression Stories

Chapter 4

Cliff

An Interstellar Pilot and Archangel

I met Cliff, an Englishman, through email and we scheduled the regression to connect on Zoom. He was in eastern Europe and I was in San Diego, CA - yet, it was as though we were in the room together because of our great connection. We hit it off right away. He was warm, friendly, and very funny.

He was in his early 70's and I would learn that he was involved in full time work that he loved and for which he had a big passion and talent - teaching pilots to fly. He wrote:

"I have been on some kind of spiritual path for as long as I can remember but keep veering off it. I have at times tuned to my Higher Self and followed advice but not that much for some time now. I have never really trusted my connection. But now I am getting on a bit, and life options are opening up for me, and to be honest I am not sure which way to go, and also what I should be doing to find my planned path. It is never too late."

He also wrote, "I do have a pattern of blocking off my Higher Self even though I have had a good connection in the past when I was being encouraged by my second wife who leads her life being guided by the other side. I am sure all that will come up in the session."

During our interview, Cliff shared that he tends to hide or sabotage his Higher Self from appearing, which showed up during his regression. He shared that his beloved second wife, who was massively and deeply spiritual, gave him the name of C.P., a nickname for his Higher Self, meaning "Cliff's Positive." He missed her and they hadn't spoken in many years.

He also shared with me that his heart had been pounding hard at times recently because of damage caused by high blood pressure which had started to return after having been reduced to normal levels. He had curiosity about dying of a heart attack as his Mother had. And he told me that although he used to be in touch with his Higher Self, for the past 20 years, he hadn't really trusted the spiritual connection.

Past Life - Eaten by a Black Leopard

His brief past life opened with Cliff wearing brown leather sandals and a loin cloth. He was carrying a bow and arrows, waiting for an animal to come out from the bushes so that he could kill it.

Then suddenly, a black leopard appeared within striking range, attacking and killing him. Almost immediately Cliff left his body as he continued to watch the leopard eat his flesh. And somehow he found this funny.

I asked, "Looking back on this past life, how do you feel about it?" He felt sadness because he didn't know his Higher Self, C.P., better. And sadness because he hadn't been connected to the spiritual realm for guidance, a place he recognized on his return to his spiritual home.

Spirit World and his Spirit Guide

Having died, Cliff entered Spirit World and saw a distant light, half shaded. He wanted to see the Light, but it was hiding around a corner as though it were playing peek-a-boo. The light was white, and it was a like a translucent, human sized being.

I sensed this may be his Higher Self and that perhaps he was, once again, blocking it, at least momentarily. I also pondered whether this Light could be a healing spirit which had greeted him, in order to bring healing to the ghastly trauma of being eaten alive.

However, as we moved forward, this White Light was then looking at him. As the two made contact through the White Light's gaze, Cliff reported to me that there was a lot of humor! He suddenly saw the irony (in his past life) of being the one who was eaten when he was, in fact, the hunter!

The Light proceeded to share the fact that it had been trying to connect with him, even when Cliff didn't believe that the Light (and others in Spirit World) were present or with him.

The Light said, "He knows exactly how to do this. We've told him many times that he needs to turn to the Light and ask, believe, and make efforts to understand his divine guidance. There are choices to be made by Cliff. If he'll follow his intuition, all will be right."

The Guide went on to tell him that since Cliff hadn't been in connection with Spirit World, his connection was not as strong as it needed to be. He added that there's no need for discouragement since Cliff can actually connect anytime he wants to.

The Light said that Cliff used to stay connected through his ex-wife who was deeply spiritual. But after they separated, he no longer had the confidence he could make the connection himself.

I shared with Cliff that sometimes, when we're with someone who has advanced spiritual skills, we find that being in their energy field may open us up to these abilities within ourselves. And when they are separate from us, it isn't as easy. He agreed. He regretted he hadn't made more effort over the past 2 decades. I thought of the past life shown where, after his death, he felt sad about not connecting to Spirit World for guidance. But now, he clearly wanted the connection.

Then, the White Light surrounded him. Cliff said that he had been hiding from his Higher Self, or C.P. His Higher Self had been working on Cliff for years, but Cliff believed he was not chosen to connect with it. Now Cliff felt energized. Now he could speak through his Higher Self and be his own Guide.

He said that C.P. is the White Light, the part of Cliff which is not of Earth. I gathered that this is his Interplanetary name.

I asked Cliff, "Are you your own Spirit Guide?" He answered, "Yes."

Guardian angel

Cliff announced that he had a guardian angel. Just then, Cliff shared that the angel had appeared with large wings and it was enveloping all parts of him - loving, protecting, and hugging him.

The angel was a male, angelic essence who he named "Youlot." Once, in a dire situation, Cliff said aloud "Okay, you lot, if you exist, do something!" and immediately the situation was resolved, and his life saved. It was while piloting his plane, flying at night in dreadful weather, over the ocean, and suddenly all the power and lights went out. After asking for help, Cliff flicked a few switches and only the exact combination restored the power and navigation equipment. It happened just in time to save him.

We discovered that Youlot is an archangel from another realm. His essence consists of enveloping anyone, anywhere, and at any time, who needs help with guidance or protection. Throughout the regression Youlot brought in a great deal of humor.

I addressed Youlot with our questions. "Is Cliff of the Angelic Realm?"

Immediately the answer came as a "yes." And not only was Cliff told he is of the Angelic Realm, he himself is an archangel and from another universe.

Youlot also added that Cliff is an interstellar pilot. He can fly anything instantly, whether it's a UFO, a flying object, or any Earth machine.

He added, "As an archangel, Cliff guides others, when they are open to it."

We were interrupted by Youlot who spoke for others in the Angelic Realm, referring to Cliff. "He's hard work for us! When he's flying, he makes mistakes right to the edge, testing us. He does this in Spirit World as well."

Cliff said that in the physical world, he flew to the edge of its limits and allowed his students to think for themselves and make mistakes. And sometimes Youlot and the others had to keep him alive. It was a team effort. He informed me that whenever he asked for help, in a pinch, he always received help from them.

You may be thinking, as I was, "Isn't this terribly risky, unnecessary, and dangerous?"

Youlot explained that Cliff likes to keep everyone in the Angelic Realm on their toes, keeping their angel skills sharpened. (There was a lot of laughter again.) He explained that all skills need to be practiced. By Cliff making them practice their work, they became better and it also made himself work harder as well. As a teacher, he knows this to be the way we all learn best. I thought to myself, "Imagine helping angels to improve their skills!"

I began to understand how Cliff and the angels work together and at the same level, interchangeably. Youlot chimed in, agreeing with Cliff, saying that Cliff was assisting the angels by keeping them sharp and in practice.

I asked Cliff why he flew as an Interplanetary Soul. He said that, as an archangel, he can travel anywhere instantly, anywhere inside or outside this universe. (Dear Reader, I know this sounds unbelievable, but

I've had other souls tell me similar things during a regression. And one is my husband.)

Interstellar pilot role

Cliff went on to explain his role as an interstellar pilot. Within the universe, non-physical beings need to be transported to their destinations for the purpose of growing and developing.

I asked for what reason they need transporting. He explained that an entire population of souls can go to a vacant planet that has nothing and no one on it. It's his job to transport a group of souls to the planet. He added that, at the same time, he can simultaneously do this while living his human life on Earth. (Interplanetary souls, such as Cliff, are noted for this.)

He explained that souls – like passengers - have to be taken to a planet where they can develop into either plants or beings. He called these passengers "soul seeds." When they're ready to evolve and take the next step out of divine Source, Cliff transports them.

He shared that he moves at incredible speeds and still is able to transport everyone safely. I felt how deeply he carried his purpose and its responsibilities and also how he rose to the occasion with such joy.

I asked Cliff what percent of energy he brought with him to Earth for his incarnation here. He answered "30%." Then I asked what percent of his energy still resides in the interplanetary realm. He answered "70%."

While most Earth-based souls come with far more energy, between 60-70%, Interplanetary souls require less of their energy on Earth. That's another way, along with their higher intellect, in which they are more advanced than we are.

His interplanetary roles

I asked Cliff to please tell me more about his interplanetary work. He explained that when soul seeds (or entities) need transport, during the journey, he teaches and guides them in order to prepare them for what to expect, and the shock of becoming embodied. Cliff's knowledge was vast and intelligent. I was amazed at what I was learning, feeling humble and grateful.

Fortunately, as a regressionist, I have regressed other Interplanetary Souls and had also learned about them from my teacher, Dr. Linda Backman, a foremost expert on the subject, who writes and speaks extensively about the subject. These Interplanetary Souls truly deserve to receive our appreciation for what they bring.

He said that soul seeds have to be prepared. And by his encouragement, saying things such as, "Yes! You can do it!" it makes a difference. As a soul, Cliff provides encouragement, instruction, rescue, and motivation.

I asked if he had an interstellar flight route. He said that he can go anywhere he is asked to go and at any time. This is how his skills are utilized and needed.

He went on to explain that, sometimes soul seeds need to be rescued in order to be planted elsewhere.

I wondered how a soul seed rescue happened and if that would mean that the soul exited Earth through a death process. He said it did not and that the seeds were planted again to continue in a new environment without actually dying. Later on, when soul seeds are strong enough, they learn to go through the death process and experience different bodies. He added, "These souls are too young yet to go through death. That will come later."

Some of his roles are indescribable

I began making a list of the spiritual, interplanetary roles I was learning about Cliff: teacher, guide, and pilot. I asked Cliff if I had missed any other roles. Youlot chimed in saying I'd missed one, the "healer role." Cliff added his additional roles as a catalyst as well as a protector. (Afterall, he was an archangel!)

Cliff told me there was an item on an Indian restaurant menu and it was called Pakora and the description of it was "indescribable." He and Youlot both agreed that there were other roles he played that were indescribable.

He said he does what any angel does. And, when souls move out of the body at death, they can be helped by him. He can collect, protect, and assist them to go elsewhere.

Whenever he deals with baby soul seeds who incarnate and who become physical beings, he helps to protect them. He added, "Of course, we don't ever die."

The past 20 years, a waste?

I brought up the fact to Youlot that for the past 20 years, Cliff had been mostly off the spiritual path. "Was this time wasted for him?"

Youlot said, "Just because he believes he was off his path doesn't mean he's actually been off his path." Cliff added that he's been trying to learn to be a human being since he's already a spiritual being. So, it wasn't wasted. (I thought to myself. I'm here as a human who's trying to be more spiritual. And he's here as a spiritual being who's trying to be more human! I was having many paradigm shifts.)

I asked Youlot, "For what reason is Cliff incarnated on Earth?" He said that he incarnated for learning - anything and everything - and at all levels. And also to teach and be challenged.

A Catalyst

Then he shared another of his important roles, being a catalyst. I got the feeling that we could be talking for months and he would still be adding to the list of amazing roles he takes on with powerful capability. I have never talked before with a more unlimited human being! He felt I was beginning to understand him better.

I reflected that, in the beginning of our talk, he shared that he had been stuck in a 20-year rut, frustrated that he had not engaged with his spirituality, and he was wondering what his life role was.

Now, less than an hour later, it hardly seemed like the same person to whom I was speaking. He had transformed before my very eyes to his Higher Self: confident, awakened to exactly who he is and enjoying every moment of fluidly sharing it with me, and exposing his amazing talents and skills and roles of infinite magnitudes. We proceeded.

As a catalyst, he causes things to happen. (This is a lesson in what angels do!)

At this point in our session, I asked Cliff how he was feeling? He said he felt happy and confident.

Cliff then shared that his heart, which had been pounding recently and even as we began our session together, had now calmed and was quieting down.

I asked why Cliff needed Youlot since Cliff is so capable. Actually, they seemed more like good friends. Youlot explained that we all need others to support us. Cliff chimed in, "A single candle is not the same power as multiple ones lending their light."

Stubbornness prevented Cliff from his Higher Self

I asked if Cliff's self-sabotage, hiding his Higher Self from his human self, was now clear? Youlot explained, in a teasing and loving way, that Cliff is very stubborn and he could be very difficult for them to deal with.

I asked Cliff about his stubbornness and what purpose it served him.

He answered that he was stubborn because he wanted to do things in the right way. He got frustrated when he expected himself to do something like everyone else and when it didn't happen to him as it did to others. This made him lose confidence. This has been his stuck position.

An example of this is when we began our call, he said he'd just read my book, *Past Life & Spirit World Regressions, Healing through Revealing Soul*. He really hoped that he could experience things the way others did, seeing fantastic visions and big things happening.

But then he realized that he's a "knower." And this is the reason that he can't experience things the same way as others. I began to understand that Cliff doesn't visualize. He actualizes.

He said that all my feedback had been very useful, and this was one of the best parts of the regression for him. He could see that just because he doesn't see, hear, or feel the way others do, it's okay. He realized that as a "knower," this is how he validates things for himself.

As he spoke, he realized that he needed more trust and faith in his own thoughts and feelings and to stop requiring confirmation for it to be validated in the same way that others receive. His way is different. I think that he found this helpful. In fact, it was one of the biggest gains of his regression. As Earth citizens, we can become paralyzed from comparing ourselves with others and coming out on the negative side. We all do it!

Healing his heart break

The conversation continued down many fascinating roads. I'd like to share one more. It involved his ex-wife who he hadn't seen in many years. Now, she had become a spiritual sensitive and couldn't be around anyone because of her ultra-sensitivity. She lived as a hermit and said her guides told her that seeing him again would have no purpose. I sensed that he adored her still and his heart longed for her.

He and she were from the same realm as Youlot and had all incarnated over 400 times together. But, in this life, she felt their relationship had been completed. Although they could write to each other, she said that her guidance was that there was no purpose in meeting, and she intended to remain separated from Cliff.

He was heartbroken and sad and wanted to know she was okay.

I asked Youlot if he could please help Cliff with this. Cliff went on to say that, although he had many wonderful friends, he had no one special in his life to share it with. He had a longing to find someone special.

I spontaneously called on All That Is, divine Source, and all angels to hear our request. I channeled divine Love and we called in the one for him, leaving this with divine Love to work it out for him.

As we ended, Cliff told me that after 20 years of learning new ways of being human, as a result of the regression, he was now on his path starting a new chapter of spirituality and being his Higher Self.

I asked Cliff, "On a scale between 1-10, what number would he rate this regression?" He teasingly spoke slowly saying "a 1." Then, "And add a 0." We laughed and I told him it was a 10,000 for me!

Here's what I observed:

- I was in a three-way conversation with an Interplanetary Soul and an Archangel. And they spoke to me as an equal. That's a first!
- It's hard to imagine such a magnificent soul as Cliff and his capabilities. Truly, he is a gifted and advanced soul who deeply cares for others, both on Earth and universally, and he carries out his responsibilities with great joy, commitment, love, capability, intelligence, and confidence.

- I have to add another delightful side of Cliff. His humor was continually gentle, witty, teasing, joyful, uplifting, and intelligent. I found it to be always well-timed.
- It was absolutely refreshing in every way to have someone tell me objectively about their life – their roles, talents, skills, and nature - without an apology, without withholding something good, worried about what I thought or if they were being judged, and completely free of ego. Because he was so full of self-knowledge (rare!) and free of fear (even rarer!), he allowed me inside his beautiful world and shared it easily and fluidly. It was freeing and fun too. What a wonderful way to live!
- I had a paradigm shift as a result of meeting Cliff and being with him both on Earth and in celestial realms. I recalled many decades ago when I was on my way to catch a flight, driving to the San Francisco airport. The big sky was blue and cloudless. I was listening to a call-in radio show, when out of the blue, a great distance away, I saw objects moving in the sky at incredibly rapid speeds. It seemed to be a formation of aircrafts of some kind. They could instantly separate, each moving to the other end of the sky. Or they could just as instantly come back together as one. In a short while, there were people calling in to the radio show who had seen the same sight as I had. Everyone was baffled, but they were all calling it the same thing, unidentified flying objects, or UFO's. Members of my family have also seen closer versions and with bright lights blinking and whirling sounds made by these spacecrafts. My husband and I have had ongoing discussions over the years

about the possibilities of "aliens." I've noticed our great softening over the years, especially following a Native American conference, where we learned to refer to them as star people or star friends. This represented a paradigm shift within. After this regression, many more things opened up to me, creating an even greater shift. as may be happening to you as well. Now, I will never again refer to them as "they," or as strangers. Hereon it will be "we" and as friends. I have to affirm that we have some true wonder workers out there – both among us and distant - who are trying very hard to save us and at a great personal sacrifice. I give them endless thanks, encouragement, and full credit.

- Until the regression, he wasn't fully aware that he was an interstellar pilot, and he was surprised to hear this from his own mouth during the regression! The entire regression was a tremendous spiritual awakening and self-realization to Cliff. It was just what he had been needing and for a long time.
- Regarding learning to fly Earth aircrafts, he said, "Flying an interstellar craft is much easier. It is pure mind controlling matter. Think it and it happens. But the thoughts have to be pure and focused. I sometimes have trouble with that on this Earth plane."

An update:

Cliff and I became friends and emailed many times, staying in touch weeks after his regression. Our discussions were mostly about his Higher Self evolving and my encouraging him. This led to him creating a new website called Lightlink.com where he offered meditations from his Higher Self, "C.P."

Within a few months, I received an email from his sister informing me that Cliff had a sudden heart attack and passed on. He and I had been in touch just days before this. The last words he emailed to me were, "I just wanted to say I am perfectly okay." I was shocked by the news of his passing and felt a great loss. I've missed Cliff. It's not often that I come across someone I have such a deep connection with, and I'd taken a strong interest in his spiritual journey and growth, which we emailed about almost daily.

There are things that have lent me comfort.

In my work as a soul regressionist, I have found that souls of high consciousness such as Cliff, are in charge of their death. They have reported to me while exiting a past life that they left their body even moments before their body actually died. Having incarnated so many times before, they know exactly how to exit their body and to look forward to returning home to Spirit World.

They also have no fear of dying since they know Spirit World is a place of love. Often, they have reported to me, before their past life death, that they knew when it was time for them to die and they were ready. I felt this was all true for Cliff.

As I read over his regression, I was deeply grateful that Cliff had awakened to his Higher Self and had completely connected to the spiritual realm and his life purpose. His regression had been life transforming. He made it clear that his regression was a pinnacle point in his life as it explained so many things for him that his soul needed to know. When he first emailed me, 'I have never really trusted my (divine) connection," he had completely reversed this former position. Cliff had fully awakened to his spirituality.

I truly believe that, at the exact moment of his heart attack, Cliff had the power to choose where he most needed to be, whether here or in the Angelic Realm. As we discovered, he was one who lived without limits and this is what he told me was the favorite part of his regression because he knew it was true and few others knew it.

I concluded that death didn't take him. One who was without limits was in full charge. He was – and remains – an archangel and a spiritual master of his destiny.

Chapter 5

Michelle

A Priestess & Goddess of Light & Divinity

When I met Michelle there was wonderful energy radiating from her. Now in her early 40s, she was between jobs and wanted to have guidance on what direction to take.

Michelle had delved deeply into sound energies to experience deeper states of mind. She was passionate about a recent gong program where she and friends had gathered to experience the gong vibration in their hearts.

Her PhD in neuroscience helped her research brain waves. Applying this to spiritual states of consciousness was her passion. I felt excited to be working with someone with so much scientific knowledge about my favorite subject!

Michele came with specific questions:

- What were her soul's gifts?
- What was her life purpose?
- What about the upcoming job interview?
- How could she communicate with angels, guides, and her Council of Elders?
- Who was her soul family?
- Who was her soul mate? Was it her husband?

- How could she combine science and spirituality?
- How could she better communicate with animals? (She had a special connection with them.)

I hoped we could get all, or at least most, of her questions answered.

Past Life – a High Priestess

When her past life opened, she was dressed in a white robe wearing a ceremonial mask. She was alone.

I asked her to imagine a mirror and tell me what she saw as she held it up to her face. Looking into the mirror, Michelle could see that she was wearing a beautiful Egyptian mask of turquoise and gold. It covered her entire face.

As the scene continued to unfold, she realized that she was standing on top of a large pyramid. From this position she viewed green land and a city of about 200 people below.

Michelle was an ancient Egyptian priestess. She described a peaceful vibration over everyone and everything, which she helped to initiate. Part of her work was to oversee everyone's well-being and to maintain the high vibration for her community.

I asked how she was feeling as she stood on top of the pyramid. Michelle said she was feeling confident and powerful in a very calm and peaceful way.

I asked about her role as a priestess. Her job was to maintain an elevated consciousness within the entire community. The main way she accomplished this was through an altered, yet conscious, meditative state. As she spoke to me, she described energy coming from her hands and feet. It felt like waves of gentle electricity, which, through her intuition, assisted her to help others. Maintaining the mental and energetic state, she happily did this for the people.

On top of the pyramid, Michelle watched large birds, perhaps eagles or falcons, flying near her. It felt as though they were in harmony with her and even aware of her. As she felt their swirling energy, she was one with nature.

Michele reported that she was in touch with a universal energy that was soaring through her and because of that it affected everyone and all of nature. People below knew and appreciated what she provided for them.

I asked her to explain herself. Who was she?

She's "a priestess and goddess of light and divinity." As she described herself, Michelle said that the energy was increasing as it came out of her hands and feet. It caused her to feel at one with the universe. We paused so that she could feel it deeply and be able to draw on it in her present life. As she did this, she noticed a beautiful sky, grass, and people going about their lives. She felt part of them yet detached from them as well.

She was part of a universal energy.

She was respected by the people, not known personally by them, but she was highly regarded in her role.

From the sky she could see a bright golden light, its rays shining down on everyone. She could feel heaven and Earth meeting and she reported that she's a connector of this.

Scene 2 – home is a royal palace

Leaving the pyramid for the day, she stopped to pet a lamb - feeling love for him and appreciating his softness. They were both connecting with each other.

I asked if she had a special connection with animals. She said yes. Her hands on the lamb felt like an energy connecting them. She was calmed by it.

As she walked on a dirt path, she could feel a protective force around her. The people didn't notice her.

She was aware of feeling separate from the people. It felt normal.

Michelle explained that it was necessary for her to stay distant from the people in order to maintain a pure state of her energy that would protect and prevail over them.

Her spiritual teacher helped her to develop this state. She'd been doing it since a child. She had never had a strong connection with her family, having left home early in order to begin doing this work.

Scene 3 – a mystery school

Michelle arrived at a palace with large-sized columns. The palace housed a royal family and she was employed by them as the priestess.

She was the only one who held a spiritual position but there were student male counterparts, like priests. The community was an advanced spiritual community. In the palace area, consciousness was very high.

They lived near the Nile River. The pyramid wasn't like the great pyramids. These were smaller and more the size of the Mayan ones with steps.

Scene 4 – a magical wizard

It was night and Michelle was under the starry sky. She was meditating and studying with a teacher and his spiritual group of about 4 people. They were camping. An older male was the teacher and a high priest. He was like a magical wizard or sorcerer.

He wore a sapphire blue robe and a wizard's pointy hat. He had a very evolved consciousness being highly connected with the divine, similar to her gift of being connected to universal energy. He was a wise man over 100 years old, and yet in good shape. He orchestrated nature by incorporating sounds.

He was in tune with nature in ways that were natural to him. This was also similar to what she did. The wizard actively created high levels of energy and consciousness whereas she was more a protector to keep things at a high level by working with the universal energy.

How was the wizard creative with nature?

He used other aspects such as sound and energies through his hands as he also raised consciousness the way she did. The students were wide eyed and listened to him as they enjoyed his presence. The students knew less than she. They were peers, although she was his one student and they were both employed by the palace.

This was an ancient tradition that took place as a mystery school. It had been held traditionally outside under the stars, for many thousands of years. The teaching always took place, one-on-one from teacher to student, to make sure they could keep the understanding of the energies alive.

She mentioned several times that she felt disconnected personally from everyone in the city.

Her role gave her access to the teachings and it required her to maintain a certain distance from the people. She lived in a different state of consciousness from others.

When her teacher passed, she would take over the teachings. She was in her early 30's.

Scene 5 – creating a vortex

Michelle was back on the pyramid noticing her hair was gray. She was now about 80, feeling very healthy, and conducting a ceremony to bless the city. Spiritual consciousness has continued to be an important part of the people's life.

Now at this older age, her universal connection felt even more powerful and advanced. Michelle noticed the large birds flying and she could feel the swirling energy coming from the birds as the energy also came from her hands and feet. It created a vortex.

With the advancement of her unique energy, she'd learned about creating vortexes. She was now the High Priestess. The wizard teacher was gone.

Michelle had concern for the level of consciousness of the people. It had lessened. Although there was drama in the city, from anger and violence, she felt separated from it. They still respected her, but she showed concern for them.

The drama that increased had come from lack of remembering their power, love, and connection to their universe. Her goal was to be effective with bringing them back. However, she could only help. She couldn't do it for them.

Last Day - High Priestess dies

She was lying on the palace bed, aware of chaos outside the palace, which she couldn't stop. She now had to let it go. Michelle felt sad and disappointed.

She was now over 110 years old but didn't feel old. Her role was done. The world was moving to the next phase, going backwards, and she was not part of it. Ready to leave, Michelle made the choice to let go and die.

Crossing over – the world had rejected her soul

Crossing over to Spirit World, she moved away and above the battles, the palace, and her body below her. She felt calm.

Looking back on her life, Michelle no longer resonated with the world, which was headed to a new place. It felt like the world had rejected her soul. She told me that she no longer felt a part of the world and said, "My vibration is no longer compatible here."

Spirit World – arrival at home!

Michelle was aware of being in a tunnel. There was a dark purple, misty light surrounding her and pushing her upward. It felt blissful and she sensed a connection with the universe. She described the feeling of intense bliss in her heart as if she were standing in front of a gong and the sound was resonating in her heart. We paused so she could feel the deep, intense vibration and allow it to be locked into her memory.

The purple light then opened up into a golden light, which appeared in front of her. This golden light took over everything. It felt warm and like a very calm, blissful vibration that was slower than the faster purple vibration.

She had arrived home!

Her Archangel Guide - Gabriella

It felt like an Angelic Realm. From a light, an archangel with enormous wings came forward. Her wings were half open - happy, loving, and warm.

Her name was Gabriella, the feminine counterpart of archangel Gabriel. I noted that archangel Gabriel was known for his trumpet, and I asked her if the trumpet had something to do with her role. She explained that the trumpet sounds create the universe. Michelle said this evolved from her same teachings used as a High Priestess.

I noticed at this point that my client was moving her hands in the air. She explained that these were mudra hand positions which were actively moving energy around her. She knew about mudras but only understood them from an elemental place.

We asked Gabriella if she was here to be Michelle's teacher and guide. She said she was.

We then addressed some of Michelle's questions and began with what she needed to know about the mudras and sounds. It was explained to us that the mudras were opening a portal. By opening them she can begin to download more information from the Angelic Realm. This also clears energies on Earth.

Mudras and sounds had come into her path of destiny at this point. Michelle has been interested in them for a long while and they had recently become more prevalent in her present life.

We asked Gabriella what Michelle needed to know. It was explained that this was not an Earthly teaching and would be harder for her to learn in her present lifetime but was within her ability. It's harder to learn in this density but she is supposed to experience this as part of her work.

I asked Gabriella for what purpose Michelle was sent to the particular past life of being an Egyptian priestess. Gabriella said it was to remember the connection and power of universal energies at a time that was easy for her.

The work of her present life had been elementary compared to her past life. Her education on brain frequencies were meant to help spark remembrance of what she once did easily when she understood frequency and how it affected everything in the mind, body, and brain.

Michelle's scientific understanding had helped to bring her back into the understanding from 1000's of years ago. I once again inquired about her hands and what was going on with their constant rapid movements. She said she was still opening and clearing energies.

Michele explained that these mudras were opening and clearing energies for herself.

I asked if this would help awaken Michelle to her Earth work in her present life.

It seemed to be preparation, balancing the energy, to enable her to move into a less dense area. It was explained that what would most help Michelle do this is to develop the practice of energy clearing, moving kundalini. She was told to practice this, combined with her other practices of sound, energy healing, yoga, and other such things she does with her friends.

I asked archangel Gabriella how she felt Michelle was doing in her present life. She answered, "Proud of Michelle!"

It was suggested that Michelle flow. She had a resistance to flowing and sometimes blocked it. The reason she resisted flowing was because of her family's conditioning and pressure for her to be successful. This interference slowed down her entire process.

We asked archangel Gabriella for help with this and paused for this to take place. Within a few moments, Michelle reported that she was given a feeling which helped her to relax her mind and ground her. This stopped the freezing and Michelle reported that it helped her.

Council of Elders

Upon our request, archangel Gabriella took Michelle to her Council of Elders.

She described a circle of light. It was cloudy, beautiful, and golden colored. There were about 6-8 divine beings in each section of the circle. Michelle was in the center of the circle. She felt the presence of a beloved cat that she had growing up in her present life.

Michelle described seeing clouds where she saw a white golden light. She couldn't make out the structure of the divine beings.

They spoke as one. Gabriella facilitated and guided the Council visit hovering overhead.

The Council felt tall and thin. I asked her to look into a mirror so she could see her soul in the reflection. Michelle reported that she saw white flowing hair and robe. Light was coming through her skin.

Two of her Council of Elders were of the Angelic Realm and they all also represented other different realms. The other 4 had different forms, like animals. They were connecting to her heart.

One of these animals was dragon like, as the Thai temple dragons. They represented a magical, spiritual connection and protection.

I asked how these dragon-like representatives would describe themselves. She said they described themselves as ancient divine beings who serve. They were connecting to her heart.

I asked her Council, "How is Michelle doing in her present life?"

They described her as very studious. Her progress was seen as loving and breaking through. They advised her to be in the light and they offered guidance to do this by staying in a high vibration, being in nature, and being around positive people. She was advised to continue developing her yoga and her network of people as her community, and to also have fun with her husband and kitty.

It was explained that Michelle has animal guides – leopards and panthers and her childhood cat, Christmas - who often guide her and give her comfort. They were there with her at the Council of Elders meeting to keep her calm.

Michelle explained that Earth animals in her present life help to keep her calm and full of joy, helping her to understand that consciousness means that we are also one with the animals. She said we are to do them no harm.

We asked Michelle's questions to her Council of Elders.

What are her soul gifts?

They described her gifts as a keeper of energy and high vibration. The Council is helping her in her present life by making her aware of them through energy healing with her friends.

Michelle said that she felt angels.

We asked if Michelle is of the Angelic Realm. They answered. "yes."

What kind of angel is she?

She flows with nature's high vibration. She feels love when she feels her heart connection vibrate with the universe and she creates from that space.

We asked the Council how this worked. Michelle said it is difficult on Earth right now and this is why she's seeking help and guidance in the regression. There are others from her Realm who are doing this and she's in touch with one of them, who is a good friend in her present life.

Michelle explained that a lot of her previous questions seemed insignificant now. She felt that her central need was to learn how she could be on Earth to use her gifts and feel fulfilled. We asked her Council to please answer this question.

The Council said it doesn't matter whether or not she took the new job or new career. These were little things. Overall, it didn't matter. What mattered was being in the moment.

Michelle said she wished she could better understand how energies fit into this lifetime. (She looked into Reiki and didn't feel attracted to it.) We asked her Council for more guidance on her understanding of energy.

They said she needed to learn to feel, hold, and send energy. This was important to her life, whether or not it related to her scientific career path.

I reflected that with her High Priestess background and advanced methods and mudras, she was qualified and prepared for her energy work. I asked the Council to please verify this.

It was confirmed that she was developing this, and her path is one of elevation, ascension, expansion, and deepening of high vibrational energies. She agreed and said also that sharing this with others was important.

It seemed to me that Michelle had been given the big picture of why she was brought to the regression.

I asked if Michelle was also an interplanetary Soul. This was confirmed.

She experienced a past life memory of travelling on a spaceship using consciousness to guide the ship. She was one of several pilots using her energy to guide the ship. The purpose of her travel was to go to a place to be of service through the energy of consciousness-raising. This is what her soul does. She's been involved in this for millennia.

In her present life, will she come into a group of others who also do what she does? Or will she be more like the priestess from her previous life who remained isolated from others? It was explained that she will bring together people with additional gifts and ways of raising vibrations.

Is Michelle a spiritual teacher in this life? Yes. She has been working towards this and will be working more in this capacity.

I asked, "Is your science background helpful to be a spiritual teacher and energy worker?" She answered, "Yes, because of my scientific work with frequencies and knowing how to enter different brain states." (I could relate to her scientific work with brain wave states since the success of a regression depends on the client attaining the relaxed states of slower brain waves of alpha and theta.)

I asked about her Soul Family. The Council said she often works alone and with many animals. Her mom is in her soul family. (I sensed that her husband was also in her Soul Family, perhaps even a soul mate. During a regression, questions and answers are often out of order and I'm not always able to circle back to a question.)

Was there anyone in her Egyptian life who is also present in her life today? Not presently, although she said she may, once again, meet up with the High Priest from her past life in her present lifetime.

We asked her Council for guidance for her abundance. It was answered that she would feel support from her family and know it is okay to not worry about what job she is in. She sensed that she should connect with other yogis and co-create something together.

(It is common during a Spirit World Regression, after speaking with the Council of Elders, for the client to answer questions from accessing the theta brain wave, which we also refer to as the Higher Self. This is what was occurring to Michelle.)

I sensed that she was redefining her abundance, and that her richness and means to support herself would come from her consciousness which would guide what she needed to do in this life, whether through fund raising, organizing a company, a group, or an organization.

I sensed that she would have the means and ability because of her high level of consciousness. She agreed and added that she also had to work on her resistance to the flow. She still has a little confusion and resistance about this.

Michelle got a sense that her husband is also of the Angelic Realm.

I asked her Council for specific guidance right now in Michelle's life as she was in transition with her job and needed the best plan for her direction. It was verified that the Council told her to go through the process and she would be held in the best possible way, guiding her job interview and the decision she would make. They said she is never alone. They will be with her.

She said that the Council made her feel supported, empowered, understood, and loved. She also felt in awe of them. However, she never felt them completely approachable because they were so awe-inspiring.

Michelle said she felt an energetic connection to them and it helped her to know they are united and there's no intimidation.

I wanted to explore her heart opening. I asked if this was what was getting ready to happen which she sensed would be big in her life?

It was answered that this may be true and that later on, this may become her primary life.

She said her heart will become more open as time goes on. Michelle felt she could connect with the Angelic Realm more through her heart. She was working on that through her energetic practices. This would guide her.

What percent of her energy did she bring to this life from the Angelic Realm? Michelle said she brought 60%. She added that energy will rise to meet her needs. (When a soul incarnates, they leave some of their energies in Spirit World. It can sometimes be a problem if they didn't bring sufficient energy to their Earth life. However, Michelle was capable of drawing in additional energies as needed.)

As we ended the session, Michelle said, "That was wild!" We laughed! It was mind-blowing! We shared how intrigued and fascinated we were by the entire regression!

I asked how she was feeling. She felt illuminated. She realized that things were true which she had thought privately to herself.

What did the regression mean to her? She said it meant a lot to feel a connection to the Angelic Realm energy. She also felt frustrated feeling like an ancient soul who was being a toddler because limitations were all around her in this life.

She said that her husband is a calm, sweet soul and people sense a light around him. She feels he too struggles with anxieties from the dense energies. We agreed that this is a difficult time for the entire world, dealing with intense energies from the pandemic and economic fallout, as well as social reform, but that there's a great transition taking place for the better at many levels.

We're working through this time period, especially people of high consciousness. It was frustrating for her that the higher energy, which once effortlessly flowed through her in the past life, now presented a struggle for her.

I shared that since she's an angelic soul of the higher spiritual realm she could draw upon this realm to develop her energy flow. Being an energy worker, she felt almost as though she was wasting her time being in a science job, not doing the energy work.

I suggested that she chose this particular time and that we would be living in a very different world in coming years. What she is presently doing, learning about energy, is contributing to this giant transformation for us all.

The most valuable part of her session was the direct connection she felt to universal energies. Feeling these energies flow out of her hands and feet as she resided on top of the pyramid meant a lot. It had been a direct experience.

Presently, she works to understand how to use sound energy. Sound tools such as the tuning fork, crystal bowls, Tibetan singing bowls, and gongs help her to understand and connect with these high vibrations. She clearly had a passion for this.

Here's what I observed:

- Many people would love to have a past life experience as a High Priestess on a pyramid in ancient Egypt, being taught by a magician. However, her life, as I've found in the vast majority of most past lives, was not glamorous. In her case, there was no social life and little personal contact with others. It was a serious, contemplative, and purposeful life of learning, with a practice of deep devotion and service to others. She was mostly isolated, and yet her joy was derived from her spiritual connectedness to animals, Earth, nature, and community. It was fulfilling to live so purposefully and being connected to all things. She held a position of great responsibility for everyone's well-being. It was a position requiring great sacrifice.
- Michelle hadn't known that angels were on Earth or that she and her husband were of the Angelic Realm. This was a surprise. She realized her hope to connect with her Council of Elders and was delighted to have archangel Gabriella to call upon as well. Light workers need these

connections from the spiritual realm to know they aren't alone.
- Although highly educated, she is interested in science mainly as a means to better understand energy and spirituality. It was interesting to me that this passion and her soul gifts from thousands of years ago have carried over to now and are trying to be reenacted by her in order to serve the world today. Although the world is very different than the times she lived in, which were highly spiritual, she's trying very hard to incorporate her gifts today.
- Michelle's regression opens up to wide possibilities free of limitations. Her 110-year-old body was still strong with life when she passed on. Her departure was derived more from her decision to leave rather than being overtaken by death from old age. This is a lesson to us all.
- I saw no ego in her as a High Priestess. Humbly, she mostly understated her position and power, valuing only her connection to universal energies in order to help all that existed. This is an anomaly from where we live today from an ego that wants to be seen, acknowledged, approved of, and needs to feel important – as well as having many negative emotions to surmount.
- When divine principles are adhered to such as Michelle devoted herself to, they emit a powerful energy field from the individual that benefit all who are within the energy field.
- Michelle felt a strong connection to animals. She said that when she placed her hands upon animals, she could feel herself and the animal

vibrating together, creating coherence. This was meaningful.
- As a regressionist and spiritual seeker myself, it felt immensely rewarding to see Michelle experience her elevated soul self in the Angelic Realm and now feel so connected to her guides – and know that they are with her, constantly. And this is true for all of us.

Chapter 6

Heidi

An Angel of Joy
& Creator of Love Explosions!

Heidi is a woman in her mid 50's. And she is loaded with joy! She has devoted her life to her spirituality.

For many years Heidi has lived from her high heart as a healer and as one who loves to bring enormous joy and laughter to all. Heidi lived in an ashram in India from time to time, but mostly, she lived in a large city in the U.S. as a highly creative entrepreneur with many wide-spread developed talents, including comedy.

Even with all her immense joy, Heidi had suffered great tragedies in her life, especially within her family. Last year, she also suffered a heart attack.

Heidi shared that she had "20 years of tough stuff." She came with a lot of questions for her guides:

- Is the "tough life" due to her karma? What was that period about?
- Can she please receive guidance on her finances?
- Will her new creative project be successful and impactful? Is she on track for doing this work?
- What about her soul contracts with her sister and her ex-husband?
- Is it possible for her to have a 2nd soul mate? (Her first soul mate was a "twin flame" and they

were still friends but after 20 years couldn't work it out.)
- What exactly is her life purpose?
- Will she be able to move to the west coast?
- How should she approach her irregular heartbeats?
- Can it be confirmed that White Eagle is her guide?
- Will she be able to make a contribution to the world regarding humor and women's rights?

In a Spirit World Regression, many questions can be addressed and investigated. In her case, all her questions would soon be answered and more, as she is a highly evolved soul.

Past Life

The past life she was shown opened with her as a child, about 6 years old, watching a man brutalizing a child whose fingertips were deliberately sliced off by the man. The man was laughing.

She realized that he was also her caretaker. She was both horrified and terrified.

In the second scene, Heidi and the boy were now young adults. They were talking while sitting on the edge of a cliff, overlooking a meadow below. They had escaped from the man and were free.

The next scene, they were married. It was 1673 England.

Spirit World

Quickly moving through the past life, on her last day, Heidi lay on her death bed and her beloved husband held her hand. She was feeling the strength of his love for her. She died and was hovering over her body as she saw him kneeling next to her crying. She sent him a message of her love and, when she did, at that moment, he looked up and knew it was she.

She recognized that he'd been her best friend and protector during this past life. She realized he was her soul mate. The two of them had also shared great love in her current life as well. However, they were now separated.

Jesus

In the next scene she was greeted by Jesus and together they were flying with her hand in his. She cried, so touched by Jesus.

She heard a choir of angels singing. I asked what they were singing. She said it was a high frequency and it caused her to feel one with everything.

The angels were not individualized. They were a band of an infinite amount of energy. Jesus waved his hand like a choir master and there was cosmic laughter and giggling. It was good to be home!

The band of angels surrounded her and Jesus. Then he departed.

As she merged with the angels, together, they became a giant, golden energy.

Archangels

Archangels Michael, Gabriel, Uriel, and Arielle were present. They hovered above her, looking on her as though she were part of everything. Their focus was on her.

Heidi's humor appeared as she described something "fun and just silly" happening. A golden chariot arrived for her and she rode inside while archangel Michael drove the chariot on his horse as the other angels were flying inside and outside the chariot, "goofing around." She and I laughed.

She saw a glimmering city with massive white shimmering lights. Flying together as they travelled fast, they practically crash landed her golden chariot on the table of her Council of Elders. We were both still laughing. (Heidi's noted for her zany humor.)

She said, "It's Michael's thing. He likes to make a big entrance!" They were all still laughing as the chariot dissolved from view.

Her Council of Elders appeared as hairy people in robes. They consisted of 50-100 angelic beings and she couldn't see their faces (as is often the case). She said the beings were smashed together. She was hovering above them looking down upon them, larger than the group as they appeared smaller.

I asked if she knew why this was occurring. Heidi said, "I like to play games too!"

Then, standing next to them, the sizes became more proportional.

The band of angels were sitting, and she was standing. The spokesperson emerged as a result of the group merging as one.

I asked the immediate question about something that I was sensing. I asked the band of angels, "Is Heidi an interplanetary being?" The answer came in, "Yes." And,

"She's also a soul of the Angelic Realm!" This was news to Heidi.

We then began asking questions.

What was the 20-year period that was so tough in Heidi's life?

The group answered that this had been the hard part of her soul's growth. The rough times had built musculature and were important for this time. It was necessary for her to experience difficult things in order to develop deep compassion while addressing the hardships.

Is Heidi an archangel?

They answered, "Sort of. She goes back and forth. Some angels, such as Heidi, have a very high frequency of joy and laughter, and they travel back and forth from the band of angels to the archangels. It was explained that the archangels are her protectors. And, at times, she needs their ferocity.

They explained that she also travels between the interplanetary Council of Elders and the archangels. Her prime home is one of joy with the other angels that share the mission of joy. She must carry joy and, if not, she would begin to die.

Heidi learned that she is on the Intergalactic Council for Earth as a steward to help Earth and she helps through her joy and her high frequency of spreading laughter. Just then, she said, "I just got it! It's BIG!"

How did she come to be an angel?

It was explained that thousands of years ago, she made a choice to join them. She was more Earth based at the time and was unaware that she was also an interplanetary soul.

As she grew in "a realm," she discovered that she was part of the Interplanetary Council.

What is the Interplanetary Council's role?

Heidi said that, for a time and, through different periods, the Council holds the nature of reality in balance so that certain life forms don't become annihilated. They also hold space open so that souls can come through and do their soul work successfully. The Council feels that when souls don't get it, however, it is sad.

What is her role as an Interplanetary Council member?

She participates in creating and holding a certain frequency for others to evolve and by holding it within herself, others have the opportunity to evolve. Heidi's a space holder to support the evolution of souls. She said that in doing this, she isn't separate from anyone.

She returns to the Council in-between her lives on Earth or elsewhere. This Council acts as the "intelligent fuel" that is given from love at the Angelic Realm. Love is the fuel that focuses their intelligence.

How can Heidi address her finances at this difficult time?

They explained that it takes courage for her to express her own soul. She most needs to be herself and to tell her personal story while expressing her zany laughter and humor, without concern.

She had an idea of this writing project being a zany comedy. She also knew that she had to give an important teaching within it to free women from the gender bondage that they carry. She knew that this project would benefit all others who suffer on Earth. It's a big calling.

The Council informed her that she just *graduated* by finishing her first work and in her own voice.

Family tragedies had brought her to the point of no longer caring about what others think. Her heart had to be broken into pieces. The Council was happy about the choice she made to create her writing project, speaking from her own voice. This was the mission all along, as Heidi had intuitively felt.

Of course, this is one of the hardest things for us to do, to be transparent about who we are, even though we may be laughed at, criticized, judged, and dealing with people who think we're wrong. Coming out of this hiding place requires an enormous amount of courage. Most of us - in past lives - have experienced punishment or even death for speaking up and being visible. We tend to carry over these trauma memories for our survival.

Heidi had a lot of tragedy in her life.

- She had been married to a very abusive man which ended in divorce.
- She tried to prevent her beloved sister, many times, from committing suicide from overdosing. In the end, her sister died, accidentally, as her life had just gone on the upswing. It was heartbreaking!

- Heidi's precious nephew died suddenly, and the entire family took it very hard. Her mom suffered great depression.

Heidi had been the fabric that held her entire divided family together through all the hardships, even while they were not so appreciative of her sacrifices, love, or efforts to help them.

Just then, Heidi realized at this point that her entire family had come into the Earth experience with a dark cloud which manifested from time to time.

Is it time for Heidi to have financial prosperity?

A lovely answer came in. "She'll always be provided for. She'll only do what's most in her heart. She will be helped by support on Earth and there will be divine aligning which will assist her. Her creative writing project will present great opportunity.

I asked if this would occur within coming months? It was confirmed that there is a producer but that coming into production will be a longer process. Her other creative work will sustain her until the bigger guns come in. The energy will build momentum first.

It was explained that her Council has been urging her to do this and to gather the tribe that will birth the baby of her writing project. It takes a tribe for support and a gathering of resources which will involve 100's or 1,000s of others. It will evolve.

Heidi needed time to launch other creations. She would be sustained and even unexpected gifts will come to her. No avenue would be closed! Her gifts can just be there (as though they could arrive without effort on her part.)

The Council addressed what had been the big part of the problem until now.

Part of what she came here for – the need for courage – has been very hard for her. Being a woman and so dissuaded from her magnificence as a child growing up, she had to overcome this as well as all the ways that the human experience minimizes a woman. Overcoming this has been a monumental task.

As her way of giving back, she speaks to all who have suffered the same things.

Is Heidi on the verge of prosperity?

The answer came with a resounding, "Yes! She won't have to worry." The hardest part has been mustering the courage to speak her truth and to rip off the veil of the cloak of shame on many sides. She was conditioned by her upbringing.

There was much to overcome in reconciling who she is within herself.

- Who she was taught and raised to be as a young girl
- Who she was taught that she needs to be in others' eyes
- The unfair standards of measuring women by their weight and appearance and many other superficial ways, had to be overcome.

She was shown that she chose to come at the time of Ammachi, or Amma, in order to raise the status of women and children. Amma is a global Hindu spiritual leader, guru, and humanitarian, who is revered as a hugging saint by her followers. Heidi has spent a lot of time with Amma at her ashram. I asked if Amma knew of her joy and laughter. Heidi told me that Amma often teases her when she hugs her.

The reason Heidi was shown that particular past life.

When I asked about a soul mate, Heidi began talking about the past life she was shown. She shared that she once had a fear of dying alone. In the past life, she was shown how loved she was to the very end. The brutality of the man who we met at the beginning of the past life neither limited nor defined her. It was for this purpose, seeing how loved she was, that she was shown this particular past life.

Do I have a soul mate?

This opens a big discussion about soul mates. Soul mates don't always wind up together as lovers or spouses though pop culture promotes this idea. Your soul mate can play any number of important roles in your life – a mother, father, spouse, brother, and such.

The purpose of a soul mate relationship is to support each other's souls on their journey to ascension. Sharing a deep bond, they are mostly interested in being helpful towards the business of each other's souls moving forward in spiritual ways.

It's possible to outgrow a soul mate if your spiritual path is on an ascended trajectory such as Heidi's. For more on this subject, see my book *Soul Mate Love, Inside Secrets from an Authentic Soul Mate Couple,* co-authored with my husband, Scott.

Scott and I are "twin flames" and after receiving over 100 Spirit World Regressions, we have tracked our consistent lives together in multiple ways, mostly in roles married to each other or love partners who didn't ever come together. Depending on what we were trying to accomplish in a lifetime, and what we most needed to learn, we brought in each other accordingly over lifetimes.

Just as a soul mate may change over lifetimes, depending on the greatest needs of your soul, a Spirit Guide can also change depending on what your soul is currently working on and the type of help you most need to advance.

Heidi is one who is vastly interested in soul advancement.

The Council of Elders spokesperson said there was potential for a future soul mate to come into her life. Heidi had been aware of this intuitively. They informed her that she's no longer able to enjoy the company of a man other than another Interplanetary Soul, like herself, since there's no one else that can create a love explosion in that way. However, Heidi hasn't known anyone, besides herself, who has that quality.

I sensed that Heidi had outgrown her boyfriend of 20 years who she thought was her soul mate. Now she had risen to a new spiritual level and higher vibration but her former boyfriend had not done this level of soul work. A new soul mate necessitated someone of a higher spiritual calibration.

To what extent is a future soul mate possible? (on a scale between 1-10, and 10 being the highest).

The council said it's an 8.

Why is it an 8 and not a 10? Is there something we can do to make it a 10?

They suggested she not rely too heavily on anyone else right now. She knows, of course, that she needs to have fun and she's doing better at finding joy wherever she is.

They said they rated the possibility at an 8 because there's a way to go. Patience is a virtue. They don't want anything to interfere with the birth of her creative project. Her soul mate is a little way off yet.

Can I help her to bring in her soul mate?

They said that I can speak to her about the loveliness that Scotty, my husband, and I share. And remind her from time to time what it feels like to be married to her narcissist ex-husband versus a loving soul mate like Scotty. The difference is quantum!

She knows the negative side, but she hasn't yet carried love on the quantum side. Her ex-boyfriend, who she felt was her soul mate, was very hard for her to let go. The two shared many past lives together. The Council indicated that they had urged her for the last 7 years to let him go. He carried every possible seed of love within him, but he hadn't matured or realized his potential. Heidi said she had finally accepted this and was able to let him go.

Are her family agreements almost complete?

It was answered that she remained here on Earth as other family members made their transition.

She chimed in that she and her sister, who recently died, continue to be in touch while her sister is on the other side. It was revealed that they are soul sisters, are from the same planet, and will travel together forever. I asked what her sister's role is in Spirit World. Heidi shared that her sister continues to develop her creativity and now has a view of the entire world for her use as a mystical poet and lover of Jesus.

What about Heidi's nephew?

He's in a peaceful place in "the beloved realm."

Being a young adult, was it his time to leave?

They explained that there was a possible window and he took it.

What about Heidi's contract with her ex-husband who was abusive?

The Council explained that this was her entry into understanding the pain of women during this time on Earth. It's hard to have the fire of service without the light of understanding. Her light of understanding pain as a woman had moved to a *knowing*.

I asked how, in this instance, *knowing* was different from understanding.

It was explained that *knowing* has a high spiritual frequency which heals just by its presence. The look of someone who's endured women's pain can heal you just by looking at them in the eyes.

Everyone who endures doesn't necessarily "know." They have to have intention for the contract and also have desire to experience and integrate the lesson. Then the knowing comes.

What is Heidi's life purpose?

Heidi is an angel of joy! She's of the Angelic Realm. She has come to stay in joy no matter what the Earthly circumstances are. This is both her gift and her challenge. Now that she has courage, she will be rewarded on Earth while she's here. Part of her life purpose preparation has been enduring the last 20 years. Now she will see the fruits of her labor.

How many past lives have she and her ex-boyfriend, a "twin flame" soulmate, shared?

The answer was "Adam and Eve. Does 7 million ring a bell?" As usual, humor was in play with Heidi!

She learned the futility of planning things on her own. Now she has the wisdom of being carried by those in the Spirit Realm.

Will she be given the means to leave her city and go elsewhere?

When she sees the progress of her artistic pursuits growing, she'll have outgrown her city. She may move more freely, coming and going from where she is, then perhaps, she will leave altogether. She has done nothing wrong by staying where she is.

Here's this Spirit World regression theme. Heidi's had to learn that the only way to progress is not by leaving her town but by learning to be herself. This has taken great courage. She's had many opportunities to do the "old school" way but this wasn't the mission. She used to doubt this but now she knows better.

Heidi has the gift of mediumship. Should she pursue it?

She doesn't need to do more than she is already doing. More is not required.

How is Heidi's heart condition now?

With the heart spasm last year, which hospitalized her, the doctors called her condition a "heartbreak syndrome." Heidi had much heartbreak and loss.

The Council went on to explain that her heart condition is now healed. Her intuitive and spiritual response to the heart attack was that it was a warning to practice being a witness to things and stop carrying the pain of others. This had proven to be helpful in her recovery.

She shared that, "The Council loves and celebrates my Mother Love within, advancing me all these years." (How beautiful, I thought!)

Is White Eagle also your guide?

We heard from the Council that, as a steward of the Earth Realm, which she is, when she feels she needs Mother Earth's wisdom and protection and to connect with her Earth ancestry, White Eagle is her doorway and protector. He is available as needed.

Will Heidi be able to make contributions?

We were told that she already has many ideas for this. They used a metaphor to illustrate an example. They showed Heidi a tree trunk and said to think of it as her play. Her writing was represented by the tree's roots which would represent the change in her destiny. Without her commitment to write the play and leave all other urgings behind, it would not happen.

They showed her the tree's branches, revealing that they would flower. And when this happens, she will be able to contribute in ways such as performing comedies, singing at orphanages to help women and kids, and more.

They spoke of an earlier play which she wrote, and which looked promising to a producer. However, she pulled back, not feeling right about it. The Council said it had been a test. She needed to speak from her own voice and not write about another's life.

Speaking joyfully about her own play, they added, "Your high frequency will be masked in the most ridiculous costumes!"

Does the Council have anything else to add? They want Heidi to remember love and to taste it, by recalling all the ways that she can remember it, and to remember her soulmate love. The frequency of soulmate love is extremely helpful, and they have been reminding her to sit in that frequency, look into this picture, and pull it into her.

The Council acknowledged that now she could trust her mission. They advised her to spend as much time in meditation as possible. She feels the difference when doing it. Otherwise, all her problems tend to be solved by using her own energies and this has proven to be exhausting.

Heidi shared that she's felt more peaceful by turning away from the material picture and receiving infusions from Spirit World.

Can you help me to quantify her magnitude? How much magnitude does Heidi have?

Sometimes off-the-wall questions come to me during a regression such as this one. I go with my intuition and ask them each time. The guides know what our questions mean and answer accordingly.

They said that, as the night sky opens and the galaxy shows its spray of stars penetrating and bursting forth an infinite amount of light, its burst lights up everything much like a shooting star. As the shooting star hits the surface, it explodes, spraying infinite pieces of its light of expression, which fills the entire Earth.

Have you ever heard anything so beautiful? I thought it perfectly suited my friend, Heidi, who explodes with love and joy!

See? Her guide knew that my question was asking to explore any of her bigness and greatness that we hadn't yet touched upon. They gave it – her soul was like a shooting star exploding and spraying into infinite expressions of light, filling the entire Earth. Heidi does this with love.

Here's what I observed:

- The regression held a strong juxtaposition of being able to discuss Heidi's role from the Angelic Realm and having soul mates and sitting on an Interplanetary Council, while also addressing her nephew and sister's tragic deaths, her finances, her tough life, relationship contracts, her writing project – and much more. Heidi even commented at one time how we were

able to do this, jumping from a high Spirit Realm to our human realm of troubles.
- Knowing Heidi through many life tragedies, sadness, and tears, this regression took me by storm seeing her spiritual capacities absolutely confirmed by herself and her Council, as well as the *felt* powerful spiritual descriptions and energies she carries. These latter far outweigh a torrent of years filled with hardship, struggle, heartbreak, and overwhelm. She had faced an avalanche of downward gravitational pulls over many years. Most could never get up from so many tragedies. I marveled how only an Angel of Joy could pull off this type of momentous buoyancy. And I felt incredible joy to see her receive a full array of gifts from Spirit World and herself fully engaged as one of its amazing angels! It all made perfect sense! And I'm sure it would to anyone who knew her.
- For years, Heidi and I have discussed her soul mate and we have called him in prayerfully. This is why I took such great care with her Council of Elders to inquire diligently about her prospects. This was an opportunity to understand if there was hope and a potential soul mate for her. I think she felt encouraged.
- I was grateful that the Council brought resolve to her ex-boyfriend for whom she agonized over the years. Their explanation of him not having the mature seeds for love would have saved her years of longing, hoping, and wishing for him. Now, it brought sweet closure.
- I caught a glimpse of Heidi's soul in the words that were used to describe her magnitude: an

exploding shooting star and a spraying light of expression which fills the entire Earth. Earlier she described herself capable of a love explosion. I love pausing to take in all of this! When have you ever heard such a description of someone? And, yet, we are often surprised hearing marvelous descriptions of our soul during a Spirit World Regression. There is greatness within us all, but we must discover it and try to live from it

Chapter 7

Larry
An Angel Clearing Regret, Guilt, & Deep Trauma

Larry greeted me and appeared as a clean-cut heavy-set gentleman, maybe in his late 40's.

When he told me that he'd been devotedly meditating twice a day for several years, I felt immediate assurance that he'd be able to go deep and uncover hidden information about himself.

However, he warned me that he was there to see if he'd ever had a past life, and he seemed to seriously doubt it. I felt confident that he would have his doubt removed quickly once we began.

In the interview, I appreciated his transparency. He spoke about a religious school that he'd attended while in his teens. It was strict. He and a couple of his friends wound up questioning the priest about some of it. I think it was a moment when he broke rank and no longer followed the religious ideology he had been taught.

We both felt eager to get started.

Past life

Larry saw himself as an American solider wearing a WWII helmet, with a brown beard, brown hair, and brown skin. On the upper part of his arm, his shirt bore 4 stripes, as in a sergeant ranking. He led several other soldiers with him. He knew 2 of them from his current life. They went to the same boarding school with him in their teens.

Dressed in uniform, outside, looking up a hillside, Larry had a nervous expectation. He was holding a gun. It was 1944 and he was part of the Allied Forces.

Just then, some snipers shot at them. One of his men was hit and they quickly escaped and headed to a hospital.

Larry saw his injured friend on the table at the hospital while the medical staff tended to him.

Scene 2

It was now winter. He and his 3 remaining men moved through an orchard in Belgium, trying to stay safe and alive as they considered entering a farmhouse on top of the hill.

Arriving and standing at the farmhouse door, he and his men smoked as he considered whether or not to knock. Feeling protective, Larry didn't want to engage whoever lived there in the war. His other 2 men felt the same way.

Once Larry knocked on the door, they received a warm greeting and were invited in to hide in the basement where they would be safe. There was a mom, dad, and a child.

Very soon, the little girl warned them that the German soldiers had arrived in an armored car.

Larry made the decision for he and his men to go quickly, leaving from the back door. They ran down the hill into the woods. It was dark, wet, and cold.

Moments later, Larry heard the Germans shooting the people in the house! He reacted by running back to the house and shooting the Germans, all 5 of them. He and his men were very upset that they had placed the innocent family at risk. They stayed to bury the family in the snow.

They went to the barn hoping to be safe for the night. Larry didn't want to. He was very concerned for their safety as there could be more German soldiers coming. Although Larry was nervous, he was a calm leader, always calculating every move, every moment. Danger was everywhere. He wanted to follow his instincts about their protection. But the others wanted to stay for the night. Larry took the night patrol and the other soldiers huddled to keep warm and sleep.

Scene 3

The next morning, more American soldiers arrived and questioned them about what happened. He and his men lied, saying that the farm family was already dead when they arrived. They needed to protect themselves as they were already in a state feeling great duress.

They left together in a covered truck.

Scene 4

They arrived at a port to board a ship, headed to England. British soldiers were also on ship. It was Cherbourg Port.

Once in England, they boarded a train. He didn't care where he was going, he was just relieved to be safe.

Larry wondered if he was going home or being reassigned. He waited to hear.

Next, he saw himself on a transport plane, going back to the French-German region. He immediately worried he would be killed.

Last day

Larry was hit by a powerful, large tank shell and he was evaporated and blown up. His body was completely disintegrated when it exploded. He described carnage around the scene. One man was cut in half. Another man had his guts hanging out. Someone was screaming. Larry was totally traumatized.

Crossing over

Through a foggy light, Larry looked back and felt sad for the farmhouse family. He felt responsible for making the decision to knock on their door. He deeply regretted letting them down.

The shooting was senseless. The Germans even shot the cow. Larry felt terrible about all of this, even about the cow being shot. He grew up on a farm and had a cow. It felt sad.

Spirit World

When Larry entered Spirit World, an Egyptian guide named Hathor greeted him.

Hathor immediately told Larry that he'd done the right thing. And that he couldn't hold any regrets, telling him, "Let it go. It's not your fault. You're not responsible for what the Germans did."

Larry began to feel relieved, like a weight of heavy bricks was being lifted off of him.

He was eventually able to let go of the trauma and he was returned to revisit the farmhouse. First, he released regret over the cow. Then Larry saw the people in the farmhouse. The dead dad was slumped over and told Larry "It's not your fault."

Then Larry said goodbye to the farmhouse woman on the floor with blood all around her. He watched as the blood went back into her body and she thanked him for his kindness. The entire family was dead.

Visiting the farmhouse and seeing them again helped him to release his regret and guilt. Then he floated away from the scene.

Spirit Guide

Larry was greeted by "Sandor," his Spirit Guide, whom he described as an old man with white hair dressed in a medieval-style white cape.

I asked Sandor if Larry had brought trauma into this present life. The answer was "yes."

I asked, "How long has Larry carried trauma in his past lives?"

Sandor said there was one instance in early 1800's where he saw his buddy drown and Larry watched helplessly. They were both on the same boat.

The other instance was from his WWII past life. Both instances were now cleared from trauma.

I asked Sandor, "Has it been since the early 1800's that Larry has carried trauma in his life, including today? About 200 years?" Sandhor said, "yes." I continued,

"And is it completely cleared now?" Sandhor said, "yes."

I asked Larry, "Do you feel all the trauma from the past 200 years is completely cleared now?" He answered, "yes."

I privately felt such joy over this healing!

Changing the subject, I asked Sandhor, "What is Larry's life purpose?"

Sandhor answered that Larry was involved in solar energy. The planet is dying and Larry is making a contribution.

Larry was told there would be an opportunity for him within a few months. Sandhor warned, "Be cautious. Don't take the first offer, though it is the money offer. Wait. There'll be another offer right after. And that will be the one you're supposed to take."

I asked, "How will Larry know? Will you give him a way of knowing?" Sandhor said he will make Larry aware at the time.

I spoke of Larry's soul qualities of protecting and safeguarding others. I asked Sandhor if these were his major soul qualities? It was answered, "Yes, these are your qualities." Then Sandhor volunteered, "Choose your path wisely."

I told him that I sensed that Archangel Michael was part of Larry's spiritual guidance, since Michael is the great protector, keeper, and guardian. I told Sandhor that, earlier that day, before meeting Larry, I'd sensed Larry's guide.

I asked if it was archangel Michael who I'd felt earlier that day. Michael said, "yes."

I asked if Larry was of the Angelic Realm. We were told, "Archangel Michael knows him and looks over him."

It ended there.

After the regression, I asked Larry, "How do you feel?" He said that it had been a vivid experience and it confirmed that he did have past lives. Larry was surprised at the death scene - how it felt to die and what had happened as he stayed there watching after he died.

I shared that he had released deep trauma that he's carried in his soul for the past 200 years. I commented that Larry tends to take on the role of a caretaker and protector, to take care of the needs of others.

Larry agreed and gave several examples where people had worked for him for 8-10 years and, when he left the job, it was a big deal for some of them, who called him afterwards to express their gratitude. For the past several years, he'd also protected a couple of women from a really mean boss.

As Larry prepared to leave, he reached for the door and said how exhausted he was, as though he'd just played an entire game of football. I asked if it was like he expected. He indicated it had been "mind blowing."

Here's what I observed:
- The regression was far more than Larry dreamed. When he arrived, he was curious to learn if he'd ever had a past life - and seemed to doubt it. It's good that he followed his

curiosity. Larry left having experienced a whopping, detailed, vivid WWII experience of being an American soldier in Europe who exploded from a tank shell. It was shocking and surprising.

- Larry was a large, somewhat heavy man. I wondered if by releasing 200 years of trauma he would eventually be able to drop the weight. When he was in Spirit World and the guide was helping him with the "weight of regret and guilt," he described a weight like bricks being lifted off him. He'd carried that weight for 200 years! Now it was gone. I don't think he was able to fully comprehend what that felt like or meant, other than the immediate moment as it was lifted off from him. I could hardly wait for him to live his current life without having that mental weight. The trauma had left his nervous system, his energy field, his body, and his core. He was restored to living without the awful burden. It was a tremendous success.
- When we touched on his life purpose and that there would be an opportunity coming soon, he seemed to be already at his limit of deep mind-blowing information, unable to process any more at the moment, though I sensed that he took it in.
- I sensed that, until this regression, Larry had a tendency to think of himself as a football player and he identified with his job. Although he was aware that he had great tenderness towards others, especially ones who he looks over and protects, I felt he may have expanded his view of himself as a result of the session.

- Even though I didn't receive a direct answer to my question about Larry being of the Angelic Realm, his Master Guide was archangel Michael. I felt Larry had a strong association with Michael through his tendency of protecting and guarding others as he did during WWII and even in his present life. I sensed that he was just beginning to awaken to his soul and to his Angelic Realm.

Chapter 8

Wendy

An Angel Healed
Of Past Life Trauma

When I greeted Wendy, I felt her angelic nature, her generous kindness and respect to me, and her caring heart. I wanted to know her.

Here's how our interview began.

I learned she had several things that she wanted to find out. First, she wanted guidance on her intimate relationship with her boyfriend. Should she break up with him? If so, could she do it without hurting him? She expressed the sadness, grief, dread, and hurt she felt in her chest whenever she broke it off with him over the past 2 years.

In addition, there was also hurt that she felt in her stomach and it made her long for a connection to God.

I asked her to imagine what color the sadness was in her chest. And what color the hurt was in her stomach. The colors in her chest were black brown and maybe a dark blue-like denim. The color in her stomach was red.

I asked what colors she needed in order to release these colors. She answered soft pink, white, and perhaps marigold yellow.

Then, she shared her intentions with me for the regression:

- Bring healing to her chest which carried great sadness and grief
- See how her past life was affecting her now and if it was blocking her.
- Identify and break old cycles
- Learn how she can help others
- Learn how to best grow and be better
- Learn how to reach her full potential

Past Life

Her past life opened where she was around age 14. It was night and Wendy was hiding in a closet to protect herself. She had on a nice dress and was barefoot.

When her dad found her hiding, he was enraged, yelling as he pulled her out of the closet. She screamed and was scared. His intention was sexual. She was violated. Afterwards, she said that she was bleeding down her legs.

I asked if this had happened before. She reported that it had been occurring since she was about 5 or 6 years old.

From the beginning of her past life regression with me, Wendy cried. She didn't stop for a very long time as we proceeded to review this very tragic life where she could not escape.

Scene 2

The next day, she was outside in the yard, which was adjacent to a forest. Looking back at the house Wendy thought of how much she didn't want to live there and wanted to run away. Her gaze turned to her brown horse standing there. He was looking at her. As she looked at him and also petted him, she felt peace.

Scene 3

I asked how she was feeling after the previous night of violence against her. Wendy shared that she felt lonely and broken. There was pain in her chest.

I asked her to take an aerial view of the house and to please tell me if there was anyone else in the house living there. She said her grandmother lived there and was in the kitchen when she heard Wendy screaming. Her grandmother didn't care about what had happened.

There were quite a few other scenes which revealed how alone she was except for the garden and the horse, which were her refuge.

Regarding the rape, I asked where she was feeling the trauma and horror in her body. She answered she felt it in her lower stomach.

Many times, feeling desperate, she thought of saddling her horse and running away. But she decided to stay. Wendy had little choice since she had no money or means to leave.

She became aware that her dad's rage was probably associated with alcohol. There were other times when he was kind to her. Feeling unempowered and hopeless, running away was continually on her mind. She never made friends.

Wendy had been robbed of her childhood. She was the victim of her father's perpetual abuse whenever he was drinking. She only wanted to be loved! Yet there was no one to love her. This was her unfulfilled longing. Wendy had now been crying since the beginning of her regression. It was very painful and sad.

At one point, she said she felt great anger. It was located in her chest and head. She wanted to yell.

We skipped forward. Wendy eventually escaped her tragic home situation. Now in her 40's she returned to the house when her dad was dying. She felt like throwing up with disgust as she entered the house.

When she looked at her dad in the rocking chair, she realized he could no longer hurt her. She had come because she still loved him and wanted to see how he was doing.

During the regression, as she recalled all the things he did to her, she sobbed uncontrollably. Though he had been violent against her and caused her heartbreak, still, he was her only family and she cared about him. As she said goodbye, she found herself feeling sorry for him. This was her closure.

What happened in her past life

Although Wendy went through the earlier part of her life alone, she managed to marry someone, in this past life, who was kind to her. She said that, as she looked at him standing in their kitchen, she felt happy. And as she saw their 6-year-old daughter, her heart was filled with love for her. It was mutual. She realized that she was finally loved!

The main subject of her regression was to address and clear the past life trauma. Although, after years of struggle, she finally wound up with love and happiness, the trauma remained deeply embedded in her and carried over to future lifetimes.

She learned that the extreme trauma from the past life had its origin in the mid 1800's and the trauma carried over into another 7 lives on Earth until today, where she continued to carry the trauma in her chest and her lower stomach area. She had suffered this trauma energy for almost 200 years!

Last Day

Wendy returned to her childhood yard adjacent to the forest. Now in her 50's or 60's, she was looking at the trees as she had often done growing up. She reported that she felt blood on her hands. Now kneeling on the grass, she looked at her wrists and realized they were slit.

I asked how she felt. She said she felt relief that she could finally be free. "It's finally over."

Crossing over

Wendy found herself slowly floating above her body. She was still feeling sad. It had been a sad life. She said that she had slit her wrists in the garden where she always found peace. She was ready to leave her Earth life.

Spirit Guides

Floating away from her body, she was accompanied by two beings. One was named Gabe who was on her left. The other was Monica, on her right. They each held one of her hands as they led her floating forward. Wendy was still crying from her sad past life.

However, she was starting to feel curious about these two guides. The three of them arrived at a shiny silver gate with two pillars. They stopped.

I asked her to tell me a little about Gabe. "What is his full name?" She said it was Gabriel. He wore a white robe and had wings that came out of his shoulders. They were not spread but were held in a down position. I asked, "Is this archangel Gabriel?" She nodded.

I asked about Monica. "Does she also have wings?" Wendy answered yes. She was about 6 feet tall, angelic, with long light brown hair. Her face was sweet, calm, nurturing, and loving. She had been guiding Wendy. Monica accompanies archangel Gabriel.

They opened the gates as the 2 angels held Wendy's hands. She felt anxious as they went past the gates to a hall in an open space.

Council of Elders

They entered an area where she saw a long table with 7 beings sitting. Wendy referred to the spokesperson sitting in the middle as a gentleman.

Archangel Gabriel and Monica were next to her and slightly behind her, attending the meeting.

I asked her to please describe the Council of Elders spokesperson. He wore a cloak and also had wings.

I asked Wendy, "Are you in an Angelic Realm?" She answered yes. I asked, "What is the name of the spokesperson with wings?" She answered "Michael." I asked if this was archangel Michael? Wendy said it was.

She proceeded to tell me that she felt a sense of peace and calm. She sensed that they wanted to heal her.

Deeply moved, Wendy described them making a circle around her with herself in the middle. Two of the angels were holding her hands, some had their hands on her back and 2 or 3 were touching her in the front. This carried great significance for her.

She felt their love and began to feel lighter. Wendy said she also sensed fairies hovering above the circle welcoming her home with their joy and love.

Michael touched her chest. She said it's the same feeling she got when she was with her horse, whose name began with the letter "M." She felt free.

I asked if the horse had been sent by Michael or if Michael had incarnated as a horse (angels can do anything). She said, "Yes," and that all the angels who were now with her in Spirit World had accompanied her during her past life by filling the garden with their angelic presence.

The angels continued to offer Wendy healing. Several times I asked if the healing was complete. But there was more needed.

I asked Michael for what reason he had brought Wendy to that particular past life. He said, "For healing. It is now accomplished. It's up to you if you choose to heal and no longer be burdened."

Checking in with herself, she felt that part of her trauma was still lingering – burden, sadness, and darkness.

Michael repeated himself, "It's up to you, my child." Wendy asked Michael for the trauma to be lifted.

Just then, Wendy said that Michael was having her breathe in his light. And on her exhale, she was instructed to let all the darkness and heaviness move out.

Shortly after this, she reported that even the two dark spots in her chest were gone. Only light resided in her chest now.

I asked, "What do you feel now?" Wendy said, "I feel complete light." I asked if she felt any spots left. She answered, "No. It's all light."

Archangel Michael's purpose for her

Michael's main reason for bringing Wendy to the regression was for her to feel loved and healed. He wanted her to find strength to do what she is led to do in her present life.

I asked Michael, "What is it you are guiding her to do in her current life?"

Michael said her purpose is to help others. This has always been her life purpose. I asked how she could do this. He said it could be through charity and that she would be able to be valuable.

He added, "You will always find love. Others will love you."

Wendy saw her soul

Still in Spirit World, I asked Wendy to look into a mirror and describe her soul's reflection. She reported that she was shown her soul through Michael's eyes. She saw colors floating together like clouds or energies of love. As an angel, the difficult past life was especially hard on her.

I asked, "What colors do you see as your soul?" She answered, "All soft, pastel colors of pink, yellow, purple, blue, and white." These are her soul's colors and her soul identity. She saw that she was highly sensitive, pure, loving, and caring.

She described the pastel colors as shimmering with energies of high frequencies of love. "I'm all about love." This has been the theme of her soul's journey.

I brought in some of the questions she wanted answered. The first one was about her boyfriend. "What should she do?" Archangel Michael advised that she needs to be by herself and not companioned for right now.

I asked, "Is Wendy's boyfriend on her soul path?" Michael answered that he was not.

"Will Wendy have a soul mate in this life?" She was given the answer, "yes."

"Will Wendy have a relationship of mutual support, love, caring, and empowerment?" The answer was, "yes."

I asked when this would happen. (It's tricky to get these future time-related answers because the guides won't interfere with your natural free will determining your life.) He finally said, "You'll see. You'll feel as you did when the angels encircled you."

Here are other questions.

- How many lives has Wendy had on Earth? About 100 or so.
- How many interplanetary lives has Wendy had? 1,000 or so.

Her biggest discoveries

Wendy discovered that she is an angel who is part of an angelic circle of Love and that she is from the Angelic Realm. She realized how much they cared for her.

Wendy was cleared of trauma. There was no more negative sensation in her chest or stomach.

The angels were with her during the past life of trauma and have been with her throughout all her lives.

Ending our session, I asked Wendy what she most gained.

She realized that during her childhood in her present life, there were times she felt the presence of her Council of Elders, but, at these times, she wasn't sure what it meant. Now she recognized their presence.

Wendy gained insights of understanding the suffering of pain and hurt being connected to her past life trauma. She realized that she was a lot more resilient than she knew.

Wendy realized that, hereon, whenever she received intuitive messages, that she would recognize them as coming from a Higher Power.

When Wendy left, having experienced a load of trauma and a long period of heavy crying, along with meeting her angel guides and learning that she too is an angel, she was a little stupefied. It was mind-blowing, all of it. And a lot to experience!

I believed the trauma was still wearing off as the news of angels was slowly coming in. I made sure she was alert enough to drive home and she was.

The next day I called Wendy

Afterwards, I called Wendy to see how she was doing. I'd been thinking of her since she left. Because she'd experienced such deep and long-lasting trauma, I felt a need to see if she wanted my help on further processing the regression. I also wanted to give her my comfort and love.

She gave me a glowing report. I knew that the regression would be life changing for her and I was delighted she had already processed it that far.

This is the most wonderful thing that can happen during a regression. Once the client sees and experiences their guide, everything changes. A divine connection is made and actualized. A deep bond of trust is forever established. From that point on, the client realizes that, although they thought they were alone, they are not. They realize that they are accompanied by divine guidance, even angels! It's one of the greatest gifts of regression. This happened for Wendy and I was thrilled.

She told me that she realized she did not feel alone and that her Council of Elders (or angels) were still with her.

During our call, I could see that her blocks were gone. The feeling of the angels encircling her was still strong. She felt confident that she could connect with them anytime.

The regression had made clear that the young man who she'd been dating was not a good choice for her. We spoke of the importance of her using the skill of discernment so that when others come into her life, she would be able to know if they carried the angelic energies. She shared that she could test it by closing her eyes and feeling it. Then, she would know. We discussed the importance of surrounding herself with people with qualities of kindness and support so that she would be able to carry out her life purpose more easily.

Wendy told me that she shared her deep regression experience with a trusted friend, who not only didn't judge it, but she drank it in! She too wanted a regression! As Wendy shared it, she began reliving the regression and releasing all the emotions more fully. It's wonderful if you have a trusted friend to confide in and who will be your strong advocate and neither shame or judge you or cast doubt about the value of your regression.

She told me that when the Council made a circle around her, she was still struggling at that point to release the trauma from the past life. And that she was really surprised to experience emotions during her regression. She hadn't realized how real it would be.

Here's what I observed:
- Following Wendy's regression after she left, I picked up her eye pillow, and it was soaked with her tears. My heart went out to her!
- Oddly, during our interview time prior to the regression, I said the word "horse." I thought it odd when I used that word in an example. It felt intuited for some reason. Then, towards the end of the regression, we learned that the beloved horse that appeared repeatedly in her regression was sent by archangel Michael to give her solace – and perhaps was even archangel Michael himself!
- In the beginning, during the interview, she told me about the problems in her chest and stomach. I asked her to tell me what color they would represent if they were a color. She told me. Then when I asked her what the healing colors would be, which would replace the colors that signified trouble, she told me that they would be soft pink, yellow, white, and perhaps marigold. This was interesting to me because 3 hours later, we learned that the colors of her soul, her divine Self, were pastel (or soft) pink, white, yellow, and blue! This meant that even before her regression, she intuitively knew the vibrational colors that would bring her healing, and they were the colors of her soul, her divine Self. Deep within herself, she carried the color

vibration that would offer the healing solution to her problems.
- I've seen over and over that, for the most part, people who come to me are divinely guided. They find me from their intuition. They tell me they somehow "just knew" to select me for their regression. And there may have been many people and events that led them to that conclusion or to my website. It shows that no matter how complicated you think your life is, being all alone, having to find all your answers on your own, you are, in fact, never alone. You're always being guided. Your guides want you to tune in and get their messages and their guidance. They urge you to do this all the time. And they live in hopes that you'll just ask for their help and allow them to guide you to a better life. Often after a regression, my clients connect the dots and see how, at other times during their present life, they were actually receiving guidance without even knowing it at the time. Once you know what it's like to meet your guides and to be guided, it's easy to be more aware when it's occurring in your present life. This is life changing.
- Wendy shared with me that she had random thoughts and visions before now, but she never realized they were from a Higher Power. Now she would recognize them being from Spirit World.
- She told me that the regression felt more like 30 minutes rather than 4 hours. I often hear

that. Time seems to lapse in the slower Theta brain wave.
- I asked if she was surprised to learn she was an angel and part of the Angelic Realm. She said yes, but that she always had a feeling she was a healer and was meant to help others. She had always prayed to angels.
- On the phone call the next day, she said that, when she closes her eyes, she can feel the presence of the angels exactly as she felt when they encircled her during the regression. We recognized this as her superpower. I encouraged her to draw on this image often.
- Wendy said she didn't realize there was such power in colors. I suggested that she go to a paint store and gather the small paint chip cards which most represent the colors she saw representing her soul. I suggested that she paste them on a card or paper so that she would be able to look at the exact colors of her soul. I felt that this would enable her to connect with her Higher Self more deeply and to grow in this way. She showed enthusiasm for this as a way of helping her stay in her true Self.

Chapter 9

Claire
Even Angels Need Self Protection

The first time I met Claire, I sensed angelic qualities. We met virtually and did the entire regression on Zoom, thousands of miles apart.

This was one of the most fun regressions I've ever given because important spiritual information kept pouring in and it was all needed and empowering.

Claire was a healer, a medium, and a reverend - a very awakened individual. Her partner was in hospice and this was clearly a very hard time for her.

Claire was also still involved in trying to settle her divorce having been separated from her ex-husband for 16 years. Her ex had been extremely difficult and unhelpful about the settlement.

She wanted to know several questions:
- Why did she choose to have a relationship with her ex-husband who had presented so much hardship for her?
- She'd been the victim of a hit and run and left with a serious traumatic head injury with 3 years rehab. She wanted to learn more about why this happened.

- What is her role in Spirit World, in between her lives on Earth?

Claire was shown two past lives.

Past Life #1

The scene revealed herself as a woman of dark skin and very dirty hair, feet, and clothes. She was in danger. A man was pointing a gun at her head calling her, "Dirty nigger!" There were many people yelling, encouraging him to kill her. She'd been accused of stealing, but she had been falsely accused.

The man shot her in the head at her temple and she died immediately. She quickly felt pain, then darkness. Her dying thought was, "unfair."

As she lay there, and tried not to die, she felt regret as she thought of her 3-year-old son. She thought how he would go to her sister. As this was flashing through her mind, she realized that she was pregnant with this man's child. Claire was a slave and she said this same man previously got drunk and raped her. He lied to the crowd telling them she'd stolen something, while she was totally innocent. Threatened by her pregnancy with his child, he wanted her dead.

There had also been a house slave who was cruel to her because she was very pretty. She tried to keep herself small but couldn't. The time was about 1834 in South Carolina. She led a dangerous life.

Past Life #2

The scene opened when she was on a bridge with water beneath. She was standing there looking down considering jumping in to drown herself. It was very cold outside. She was pregnant, unmarried, and about 17 years old.

Claire felt caught and very frightened by her pregnancy. She was a seamstress, and, one day, a man came for his wife's things. He was older, about 28 years old and he'd brought her special wrapped candies, which made her feel important. She was charmed by him. His intention was to manipulate her, knowing how young and naïve she was. The man cornered her and raped her.

She felt confused, dissociated, and thought she loved him. She romanticized his wavy, blond hair. She herself was beautiful with green eyes and dark hair. She was from a large family and he was the first person who'd ever paid attention to her.

On the bridge, as she considered jumping, her thoughts went to how she didn't want to ruin his life. However, she jumped. I said, "Do you know how to swim?" She answered she did not. As she drowned, Claire said the water was ice cold and she heard people yelling from the bridge. Her mom was one of them and she was screaming.

While drowning, she said goodbye to her mom who was hysterical with anger and hurt by what Claire was doing.

As Claire left her body, crossing over, I asked how she felt about that past life? She said she felt it was incomplete and she regretted drowning because she could have lived. She told me she drowned in order to protect the man she loved who'd taken advantage of her. She said that there was a "seed of sacrifice" that seemed to be important. We waited for this to be explained later.

Spirit World

Claire quickly went to Spirit World. She saw many who greeted her and Saint Joseph, patron saint of a happy death, was one of them. Then, she became aware of thousands of souls who'd gathered at an amphitheater where she stood in the middle and she heard them saying, "Welcome back!" They were really happy to see her.

She explained that they were her Soul Family, her "tribe." She immediately felt the energy of Mother Mary, Quan Yin, and Jesus.

Spirit Guides

When we asked for her guide to please come forward, Chamuel, an archangel of strength and protection, appeared in front of her and slightly to the left. She described him as being very tall, about 13-15 feet, and huge. He was iridescent, appearing as shimmery colors, which included white, pink, and some purple. He had a tender smile, wore a robe, and was very loving.

I asked Claire to hold up a mirror and please describe herself in the reflection. She said that she saw herself in a garden and sparkling with irradiance of white, pink, gold, silver, purple, and green. She looked identical to Chamuel.

We addressed Chamuel with the questions Claire brought for the regression.

I asked if Claire was of the Angelic Realm. Chamuel answered, "Certainly."

I asked Claire, "How are you connected to your Spirit Guide?" Chamuel answered my question and said, "I chose her. She needed protection. Welcome back home!" Then Chamuel added, "I'm familiar with Claire today. Mother Mary is her main guide.

Mother Mary

We then turned our attention to Mother Mary who was just a few feet in front of her. I asked Claire how she felt in Mary's presence.

She said, "Love! Fierce! So powerful!" Mother Mary was happy that Claire finally realized that she was her Spirit Guide. Mary had been with Claire her whole life.

Claire described Mary as cornflower blue and she had a form that poured out white light with iridescent colors of gold and silver. These were almost blinding with brightness. Mary brought in Quan Yin, who stepped forward. Then Jesus appeared saying "It's not going to be a party without me!" His presence was also effervescing. He knew her.

I asked Mary if she was Claire's main Spirit Guide. It was revealed that, although Claire was surrounded by Master Spirit Guides, Claire was her own Spirit Guide.

At this point, Claire had been taking in the tremendous presences of these Master Guides. She began crying saying, "very tender." Then Claire's body became really hot and she suddenly threw off the covers from herself while in regression. Mother Mary assured Claire that she would be all right and that she was right there with her.

Mother Mary informed Claire that the fierceness she had was also in Claire and not to be afraid. She assured

Claire that she wasn't going to leave her and that she hears Claire whenever she prays. Claire felt a complete and expansive compassion. Mary said, "It won't be long until you are here again, and you'll be with us, together forever. Claire felt relieved.

Mary assured Claire that she could call on her for help. Then Mary addressed her fear about not being able to live through the loss of her partner when the time came. Mary said, "You'll know what to do when the time comes." She indicated that she and Quan Yin would be there with her to help.

Just then, archangel Chamuel chimed in, "Don't forget about me!" indicating that he too would be with Claire. Chamuel felt like a best friend, "very tender." He made himself really big as he guided Claire to put rose quartz around herself.

Chamuel began guiding her regarding her ex-husband. He said, "Set healthy boundaries. Don't worry. You'll be fine. This is for the good of his soul. But he won't roll over. Remember, you're teaching him."

Chamuel then established his force field around her to protect her. I asked her to please describe this field. It was a spiraling egg shaped, powerful energy that surrounded her from head to toe. She felt it.

We then began asking archangel Chamuel about the past lives shown to her.

Was her ex-husband in one of the lives? She answered, "Yes, he was the one who lied to the crowd after raping and impregnating her and he justified her killing. She and her ex-husband have had 317 past lives together!

I asked if her ex-husband was her soul mate or in her soul pod. Chamuel answered no. I wondered for what purpose she and her husband had shared so many past lives together. Chamuel said they were teaching each other.

She said that when, in the past life, he shot her, she realized her own worth and power. At that moment, she learned of her deservedness. She had also maintained her dignity when she didn't beg for her life while he pointed the gun at her. Her dignity was a strong part of her soul. However, in her present life, it's been a consistent struggle to maintain her dignity with her ex-husband.

She was informed, "He's going to pass on." Claire shared that she felt an urgency to solve the relationship. I asked if she could do it. She answered, "He won't learn." It was explained that he is a very young soul.

I asked if they were going to have another life together. It was answered that it depended if Claire stayed in her power, in this life, stood her ground in negotiations, spoke up, didn't back down, and remained compassionate and reasonable during the process of completing their divorce.

Her part of their contract in this life was to stop "allowing" because she's "allowed and allowed and allowed."

It's of great importance for her to stand up for herself regarding her ex-husband and standing up for herself is also tied to her grandkids.

Claire spoke as a *knower*, saying that by correctly completing the contract with her ex-husband, she could choose not to return to Earth for further incarnations.

I asked archangel Chamuel for what reason he had shown her the first past life where she was raped and murdered. He said it was to show her the pattern of abuse where her ex-husband took advantage of her and injured her.

It was explained that her ex-husband literally had no shame. She was given an image of her ex-husband in their present lives. He held his relationships in many compartments. All of the compartments showed him as a good guy to others. However, with her, he held Claire in a left-side compartment where he showed no shame, no culpability, and no responsibility. She lived split off in a shadowed area. To the rest of the world and his relationships, he showed compassion and humility, but what he gave to her was just the opposite. He seemed to be comfortable with hypocrisy.

It was shown to Claire that, while shame can be a corrective device in the human realm, her ex-husband had no shame. He was a very young soul and had much to learn. He hadn't yet gained the experience to learn responsibility for his actions.

It then dawned on me, with the great gap between Claire and her ex-husband, if she was his Spirit Guide. The answer was a big "Yes!" And the other guides said that she'd taken on way too much with him! She had forgotten how hard it would be and how much pain would be involved with her ex-husband as such a young soul.

Claire said, "I didn't know that angels had this problem!"

She was told by Mother Mary that she's both an angel and a light. All she had to do was be around someone and they would feel her presence of love, helping them. Claire was now crying, so deeply touched to learn these things about herself and also releasing much grief and hurt.

Claire began seeing that her grandson sees her angelic qualities and this is why he adores her. Mother Mary nodded and Quan Yin was pulsing. Archangel Chamuel said, "Yes, now you understand your connection to this child."

She was also informed that her grandchild was here to help her remember who she is. Chamuel added that it is important to remember all of this and Claire said it felt very assuring to remember who she is.

Her group of Master Guides reported how happy they were at this remembrance. They'd been trying to get her attention for a very long time! Now many things made sense to Claire.

We had to pause the regression a couple times when Claire had an extremely painful headache. We called on her guides and I channeled healing through Mother Mary until it improved each time.

Claire had recently been in the hospital with a strange blood condition. After hundreds of tests, the doctors reported that it was an anomaly and they couldn't understand why her blood wasn't performing as it should.

During her time in Spirit World, it was explained that her blood condition was connected to her ex-husband. It represented grief and unexpressed anger. It was also associated with feeling she couldn't sustain her life without her partner.

Claire recalled that, when she was in the hospital, Mother Mary had come to her in the form of a blue stone. Mary's presence caused Claire to realize she needed more help with self-care, self-protection, self-defense, strength, and fierceness. She needed to own her power!

I asked if Claire was a Spirit Guide to others. It was answered that she guides 7 others. Her ex-husband, her grandson, her youngest daughter and son-in-law and a few in the Angelic Realm. Then, as often is the case when information continues to pour in, it expanded. She realized that she is a Spirit Guide to 100's of others.

Her role is to teach love, to teach the self as the divine Self, and to teach people their God-self to themselves.

I asked how she did the teaching. It was explained that she did it through her spiritual calibration (which I assumed was exuded through her love).

Targeted by a dark force

More information came in about the hit and run accident. Claire realized that it had happened as a result of a dark force. It wasn't part of this life's contract but it was part of her metaphysics since she was an angel of light. The dark lurks.

Archangel Chamuel said he was protecting her. It was explained that because her work is so big and light-filled, the dark force targeted her. When she was struck down by the car, an angel was immediately present in the form of a homeless black man. The angel explained that he came in that form so that no one would notice him. The angel's name was Tony. Now she was about to meet him again, only in Spirit World where she was able to thank him profusely for his help, even saving her life at the accident.

Claire recalled that Tony had talked to her immediately when she was on the ground after the hit-and-run. As the car began to speed away, Tony yelled, "You must stop!" When she was on the ground, he told her, "Mom, you are fine." Although she'd just suffered a severe brain trauma, she had the presence of mind to ask, "How did you know that I was a mom?"

Looking at Tony, now in Spirit World, he appeared as a really bright golden light. Golden Light is another Master Guide. She said he was beautiful!

I addressed Chamuel, one of her Spirit Guides. "For what purpose did you show Claire the second past life where she was pregnant, on the bridge, and jumped?"

Chamuel said she had courage in that life. She experienced understanding of her worth. She had also believed that self-sacrifice meant love. She said that she has to be careful about her pattern and tendency of martyrdom.

At this point Claire said she felt like a buzzing vibration. So much information had been revealed during this session! I felt that her body was having an overload and we agreed to promptly end the session.

Leaving the regression, it had deeply impacted Claire in many wonderful ways.

Here's what I observed:

- Often when speaking with Master Guides such as Mother Mary, Quan Yin, Jesus, and others, I never know who exactly is talking. They often speak as one and they cause my client to know answers. Master Guides sometime appear together.
- Later, after the regression, I learned that archangel Chamuel's pink color is thought to take heat out of emotional stress and to restore equilibrium. Considering how much stress Claire had been experiencing, I was grateful for his strong presence with her.
- I thought of the hit and run and how this was caused by the dark forces which pursue light. Claire truly needed to be aware of self-protection and to call in her Master Guides to help her each day.
- Angels often overlook their need for protection while on Earth. I think it's because they know their immense spiritual power, yet perhaps they underestimate how difficult Earth life can be with its personal traumas, murders, abuses, harshness, and enormous inequities of unfairness. Living as a human, these anguishes can create great pain and suffering for anyone, including angels.
- In many ways, this was the best of a Spirit World Regression where you can gain a tremendous amount of information about yourself as a soul, your life purpose, and your

relationships and why things happen as they do. Much was uncovered. I was really happy for Claire!
- She told me afterwards, "Our session brought a profound remembering of my nature and my way of being in the world before the hit and run injury. I'm so grateful!"
- Claire had a grand-scale, vivid, and exciting regression! As a regressionist, here are many places I rejoiced:
    o Mother Mary told her that she had heard her prayers! This confirms to us all that our prayers are received, heard, cared about, and that we are enormously watched over and helped by our Spirit Guides!
    o Claire not only had one Master Guide, but many. St Joseph appeared briefly as she entered Spirit World. He's the patron saint of protection and courage. Archangel Chamuel played a major role in her regression, as well as other Master Guides: Mother Mary, Quan Yin, and Jesus. They caused her to feel their warmth and their love for her as well as their caring protection. I could feel it, too.
    o She realized they had been trying for a very long time to reach her and were very happy about her awakening to them.
    o She was surprised to learn that she is an angel from the Angelic Realm and was a

Spirit Guide to 100's, including some members of her family who she adored.
- Claire received a great deal of help, which made a big difference to her biggest areas of pain and concern: separating from her beloved partner, addressing her ex-husband, and knowing now how to stop the pattern of abuse.
- It was surprising for her to learn that she was her ex-husband's Spirit Guide, knowing how much she's sacrificed for him and how it's personally hurt her, yet he's made little effort towards his own progress. Her efforts felt so wasted.
- She saw her immense beauty and great power as an angel and felt known, loved, and esteemed by the Master Spirit Guides.
- She realized the importance of knowing herself as an angel and acting with angelic authority in her life.
- It was empowering for her to learn that her very serious blood condition was within her control by addressing her grief and also by connecting with her unexpressed anger.
- It was heartening when Claire had a moment where she scanned her life, viewing all the times her guides had come to her and how it hadn't dawned on her until the session.
- She awoke to the fact that she needed a lot of self-protection from a dark force.

And there were many reasons for her to practice self-protection.
- Angels have to learn wisdom from their naivete' being naturally so innocent. I felt that the session had been a major lesson for her learning to what degree she had suffered abuse, hardship, over-sacrificing, and allowing her ex-husband to continue harming her without standing up for herself. It felt like an inventory of hurt had been taken. And she had awakened to this and to the necessity of protecting herself.

Each of us can choose where we put our energy and where we invest our time, efforts, and love to bring about healing.

In making these wise choices, it's important to evaluate the receptivity and reciprocity of the person we think we are helping. If their receptivity is low, we could invest our time and energies – and heart - on those who are more open and receptive to our gifts.

In this way, someone with lower receptivity could use time to grow on their own before receiving help which involves another's effort and personal sacrifice. It's important that you are not working harder for someone than they are working for themselves. Angels need to match their voluminous giving with those who appreciate it and who will make strong efforts to grow from it.

Chapter 10

Jenny

An Angel of Freedom

When Jenny arrived, I met a lovely young woman in her early 30's who carried herself with confidence.

She was wide open to what we would find. This is my favorite attitude for a regression because many things could be free to be known without blockage or resistance.

She brought some questions to ask her Guide. Among them were:

- What is my soul's purpose?
- Why do I feel alone, misunderstood, and like an outsider?
- Why do I isolate myself so much? Is it healthy?
- How can I become the absolute best version of myself?
- Am I supposed to have kids?
- Why do I feel so connected to my dog – even more connected than with any human?
- Am I meant to be in the mountains, near the ocean, or where is my best fit in the entire world?

She shared that something is always protecting her and that she suffers from negative things she has endured from earlier in this life. She added that, "I love all of life!"

Past Life

She saw herself as a woman dressed in a lovely white dress, sipping tea in a parlor. It was the 1920's. The woman was feeling nervous and skittish.

About then, a man arrived, raging with explosive anger at her. Her response was to feel numb towards his accusations. He was denouncing her without reason. There was nothing she could do. In response to his anger, she simply ignored him. She no longer cared.

In the next scene, they were driving in a car together. While still feeling apathetic, she recalled a time when she loved him, but this was no more. She wished it would return to the way it once was, but she held little hope.

Thereafter, her life was spent mostly in isolation, yet she found that she was content with her own company, just as she is today in her present life.

Last Day

Now alone, about 85 or 90 years old, she thought of her life. It was a complete waste. She lived with her husband's complete control over her. Jenny felt disappointed knowing she could have chosen a more fulfilling life. She died with very little effort.

Spirit World

Once she passed, she began floating in the clouds. When we asked for her Spirit Guide to come forward, she described a very strong and powerful, radiant presence of gold light. It surrounded her. This was her guide. We called it Golden Light.

She recognized that she'd had this Light with her during her entire current life.

Jenny felt tingling with Golden Light as it shielded her and she became untouchable. She also felt light and airy. This is how she would recognize Golden Light as she went about her current life – the feeling of being light and airy.

We asked Golden Light for what reason she was taken to that particular past life.

It was explained that the past life was given as an example of why, years ago, she got rid of a lot of people in her present life. From the mistake made in the past life, and that was repeated earlier in this life, she learned to choose better people.

In her present life, at the time she realized this important lesson, she had been dating someone. After she broke up with him, it was just 3 days later that she met her wonderful husband who she's been married to for the past 5 years. It was as though she had an immediate reward when she learned her lesson about choosing quality people.

From seeing herself in her past life, she also realized that, even then, she found contentment being alone. Jenny explained that she found a lot of strength from being alone with herself. Here are a few of the things she quickly listed from being alone:

- She learned the wisdom of not allowing people to take advantage of her or to abuse her. During alone time she can more readily see when this occurs in her life and make more intelligent choices.

- Jenny has learned to listen to her own voice and be true to herself.
- She prefers to balance herself with alone time to better manage her life. What wisdom!

Jenny saw the correlation from her past life to her present. In her past life, she made a poor choice of her husband. And in her present life, she had repeated this error, allowing abusive relationships. However, she had an awakening and changed. Then she met her wonderful husband.

We asked Golden Light for what purpose she incarnated into her present life.

Golden Light answered, "to be a light for others." She then added more reasons:

- to help others in all ways that she can
- to share her abundance when she's at her best
- to be generous
- to be discerning with the wisdom she has gained and to apply it
- to share her light more generously and be more selfless
- to be true to herself as well as balanced in giving

I asked Jenny, "What is your light composed of?" She answered with a list:

- freedom
- generosity of Spirit
- giving
- heart-centeredness
- love
- wisdom

She felt she had given a lot of love to others in her present life and her tank had become empty from over giving. She hadn't used wisdom to balance her giving. She gave a lot of love to others and got hurt and even harmed because she gave to people who were mostly toxic. She was still recovering from the experience. Jenny felt she needed to spend a couple months off, or even a year, to feed her own soul so that she could return and love once again to the extent she did before.

Jenny had an enormous capacity to love, care, and give from her heart's overflow. Within her she carried a strong and powerful life purpose.

I sensed that her present life was not about karmic lessons. In fact, it seemed as though she received the consequences early on with toxic relationships, being treated poorly. Now she had learned the need to choose people of character who would appreciate and accept her love. I sensed that she had chosen her present life to arrive at her soul's highest point. Golden Light was here to help her accomplish this. She agreed!

I asked her, on a scale between 1-10, to what extent is Golden Light powerfully protecting her? She said a 20!

I asked Golden Light if she was from the Angelic Realm? The answer came fast and strong, "Yes!"

This is a point where we begin to understand her life purpose needs.

We agreed that she would need protection because of the generosity with which she wanted to give and also in order to avoid over giving. I asked Jenny, to what extent she felt ready to move into her right place with her angelic work on Earth. She answered, "A 10!"

She's had to explain to her friends why she sometimes isolated herself, wanting time alone. This was more than a desire. It represented a basic need for her. She wanted to become the best version of herself. Looking inward, reflecting on her life, and gaining a position of overseeing are essential to the success of her life purpose.

I asked, "Are you your own Spirit Guide?" She said, "yes." Even now people come to her for guidance. She confessed that if she isn't careful, it sucks the energy out of her.

I sensed that today, at the regression, marked a life change for her. It marked a time for her to move into her right place in life. We sensed it is now "her time." She was ready to trust, be directed, and follow in what was next for her.

I sensed that she and Golden Light and her Council of Elders are less like a hierarchy and more like mutual spiritual beings who collaborate. She agreed.

Following my intuition, I asked, "How did you become an angel?"

She listed a number of reasons: through worlds of hurt, pain, and suffering - while living through these experiences and learning lessons from them.

It was affirmed that she had earned her angelic status the hard way.

We then called on her Council of Elders. She described a long table in the forest. She was standing, facing the empty table. Just then, she saw a flashback of 5 individual beings sitting at the table, eating food. Golden Light was with her, on her shoulder.

There was a spokesperson sitting in the middle who was more powerful than the others. He was wearing a white flowing robe. He said simply, "Have more faith in yourself."

We paused to connect more deeply with this experience and this spokesperson. Jenny began feeling more rooted and these beings seemed to feel more familiar to her. She felt their sense of rejuvenation with bubbling energies which were light, happy, new, and fresh.

She remembered moments in her life feeling their rejuvenating presence. She also recalled from her youth when she felt Golden Light.

I asked how long the Council had been with her? She answered, "Forever." She most feels their presence when she's at the ocean and felt that perhaps this is why she is so deeply attracted to being at the ocean.

I asked if the Council had wings? She said they did. They were also from the Angelic Realm. I continued, "Do you also have wings?" She answered that she did. Her wings were fully spread wide open but the Council's wings were down.

She explained that her wings were spread wide open because she was feeling joy, love, and bliss! We sensed that she needed to soar with freedom with her wings wide open. This was a recognition point for her arrival into her spiritual power.

While an infant, her mom told her that people were drawn to her and that it was out of the normal way. As she grew up, she noticed while travelling that people were drawn to her. We knew it was because of her extraordinary angelic qualities that people felt confident and good around her. They wanted more of her! This is what she must protect herself against, where everyone gets a piece of her. She must be wise about where her energy is spent and with whom. It was something she continually managed.

I asked how she could best manage her generosity of giving. A small list was shared:

- taking care of herself
- time alone
- reflecting
- speaking up for herself
- not ignoring her spiritual needs or putting them on the back burner

During the interview, Jenny shared some questions that she wanted me to ask her Spirit Guide. One of the questions was that she wanted me to see if she was supposed to have children in this present life. The answer her guide gave was "no." He went on to explain that it was because she needed to be free to fulfill her life purpose.

If she had children, she'd devote that love, time, and energy to their needs. In order to serve her present life in a big way, she needed to be free. Jenny told me that she personally didn't feel a need to have children and this confirmed it.

Another question was to ask about her dog, who was extremely important to her. We learned that he was sent to be her support and to be her "soul therapist and companion." He, too, was from the Angelic Realm.

I asked more of her questions for her Guide to answer, "Where do I belong? Where should I live?" The answer was that she belongs anywhere and especially in a large open space so she can feel free. Freedom was one of her soul's themes – and necessities.

Another question: how could her wonderful soul mate husband best support her? He can offer her the gift of freedom – with no rules and no expectation as to when their time would be locked in together. She indicated that they have a wonderful relationship and he understood her and accepted her.

I asked about her capacity to love others, since this is so important to her life purpose. On a scale between 1-10, she said her capacity is a 25, as long as it's with the right people! That's what I was sensing as well.

When Jenny left, she intended to act by spiritual authority to begin her divine purpose. She was excited. What a beautiful model she is of a wonderful angel!

Here's what I observed:

- Jenny is a powerful angelic soul who is mostly self-guided. Because of the enormous amount of love she carries, it's of paramount importance for her to give this love wisely and to quality people who will appreciate it.
- She is aware of the importance of her being protected by Golden Light and also of protecting herself so that she doesn't over give with her love as she once did earlier in this life. In over giving to others who were abusive to her, her love and efforts were wasted and unappreciated. Now, she wanted to be wise about her energy and the placement of her

enormous giving. This is a monumental feat for a soul who incarnates from the Angelic Realm.
- Jenny showed wisdom and ability to balance herself with quiet time alone. Her inner balance was important to her. She knew her need to listen to her own voice, not allowing herself to become persuaded by others. She was only 31 years old and had already learned this advanced lesson.
- She was clearly a confident and astute spiritual being who was intent on giving richly and wisely while remaining true to herself. She was laser on this point.
- Jenny had a lot of inner self-knowledge. She understood herself and was like a guided missile determined to make her mark. I knew she would!

Chapter 11

Joanna
An Intergalactic Being
From An Angelic Collective

Joanna is a powerful, intelligent, bold, loving individual who is probably in her early 70's.

I was impressed with her prowess as a spiritual healer and we became fast friends, once we met online, through our mutual love for Reiki. She came to her regression with wonderful curiosity and an openness to connect with her Soul Family.

One of the reasons she wanted the regression was with the hope to find answers that would help heal her wounded heart since a young adult. She had only been in love once in her life, which was over 45 years ago.

They didn't marry each other, and she herself never married. Recently, after all these years, they were back in touch with each other. She wished for a bigger understanding of their relationship. Even though he is married, there has always been a longing in her heart for him. Recently, he called her. This needed to be spiritually explored.

Past Life

The scene opened where Joanna was alone, outside, in a cave-like setting surrounded by large rocks. Looking very primitive and haggardly, wearing animal skins, she was in great fear.

She felt distressed from suddenly entering a human body. The contrast was great from where she had come from as an exalted being and she didn't feel prepared for what she was facing.

Joanna felt like perhaps she had entered someone's body and together they were co-inhabiting it. She entered this past life without birth.

There were deep, dark emotions accompanying her panic. Feeling utterly alone, abandoned, and in despair, she felt frozen there, with no interest in seeking out others. In contrast, she'd arrived from a spiritual place of sharing and caring. Her mind was still sharp, but she had no control over the body which felt more like a prison.

Looking down below from where she was among the rocks, there was a green valley with trees. She wasn't allowed to go there and felt if she went there, someone would kill her. Joanna continued to address how alien she felt to herself and others. We'd only been in the past life for a few minutes and, having sized up all of this, she said it didn't matter whether she lived or died.

Joanna hurled herself off the rocks and died.

Her last thought was that her soul would be condemned. She had failed and she didn't care.

Joanna meets the dark

The scene switched quickly after her death. She assumed that she had now returned home to her Soul Family, surrounded by loving beings.

At the same time, she was wondering what the point of that life had been and was trying to understand its purpose. She couldn't figure out what she was supposed to do in that life.

Joanna then focused on a group which appeared in front of her. She assumed they were her Soul Family. However, strangely, they looked like aliens. One female figure with grayish skin stood out from the group. A high priestess, she was formidable and wore a headdress.

At that moment, Joanna realized that these beings were not from her Soul Family group. The High Priestess and her group were camouflaged to appear as Joanna's Soul Family! And they were filled with harsh judgments for the fact that Joanna had hurled herself over the rocks and killed herself in the past life. The spokesperson bombarded her with judgments saying, "What's your problem? Why couldn't you do this?" Others from the group chimed in.

Just then, Joanna saw the words "illusion" and "lesson."

Her true Soul Family

Once these words appeared, the group vanished, and her Soul Family presented itself. They acted as a Collective, speaking as one and communicating telepathically. They wasted no time explaining that the past life experience was shown for the purpose of revealing that dark judgments can color your experience and fill you with fear, mudding your purpose. Self-judgment looks much like the High Priestess. This was her enemy.

The entire past life experience was to teach Joanna to remain clear of dark distortions such as self-judging.

I asked, "Who is this Guide addressing you?"

Joanna spoke for them saying, "We are a group, a Soul Family united. We speak as one. We have no name."

They continued to explain that she needed to come to them, asking them questions, adding, "Times continue to be dark. It's imperative to remember where you came from. You can see clearly if you don't get stuck in that dark realm and you'll know it was just like that!" (referring to the experience with the High Priestess)

They continued, "Self-judgment is your enemy."

I asked if her Soul Family represented an Angelic Realm.

Joanna said they described themselves as an amalgamation, a combination of beings. They explained that they are a core essence of angelic "*ultra*terrestrials," not "*extra*terrestrials."

Her experience of having a spiritual essence of high and refined light created a shock when she entered the body of that terrified rock dweller. It was too much for her.

She received no judgment from her Soul Family. Instead, they had compassion when they felt the experience through her as it occurred. Without her having this experience, they would not have been able to feel it.

I asked if she had been a "walk in," where she entered a body that already existed. She said they call it "not signing up to go through the birth." A higher consciousness joins the body with cohabitation.

The purpose of the past life was to bravely descend in order to practice being of service to 3rd dimensional beings, but the plan had proven to be too much. She had consulted her group prior to descending, but her "fervor for service," to be able to be of guidance, was stronger than any of their objections.

I asked if being of service was a big part of her soul. She indicated it was, adding that there were aspects of her soul journey that couldn't take place without embodiment.

Many of her group feared getting stuck in a body with karma and didn't have the courage to take the plunge to descend and embody.

Joanna learned from this experience to proceed more cautiously and not so extremely. It is through her own choice and ability that she came into 3-D form, whether becoming an animal from another star system or choosing among the many other ways of entering.

Because of their shared essence, Joanna acts as her group's "liaison, the bravest of them all, the pioneer."

I asked if she was an interplanetary soul?

She said no. Then Joanna added that she was an interstellar and inter-galactic soul, which was much bigger than an interplanetary soul. Whenever she leaves a 3-D experience, she returns home to her Soul Family.

I asked what her intergalactic home was like?

Joanna shared that it was "total love, beyond description." There was complete safety, comprehension, all knowing, light, comfort, peace, and joy - much like a happy family feels and way beyond.

The past life shown was the beginning of herself as a pioneer soul. It was a time before the pyramids were built. And it did not take place on Earth, but in another galaxy. She explained that there are billions of other 3rd dimensional beings who look nothing like us.

In the past life, she envisioned herself in humanoid form, at a primitive time, and the feeling was one of despair.

How does this past life relate to your life today?

Joanna said it relates through self-criticism. From childhood in her present life she was programmed with, "You aren't enough! You aren't worthy! You can never do enough!"

At this point of her regression, she explained that she and her Soul Family were communicating from their soul to hers and they were one.

Joanna went on to explain that spiritual overachievers, like herself, are capable of great joy and laughter. Those of the light have joy and laughter, in contrast to self-criticism. This made it difficult for the criticism from the High Priestess to stick.

In her present life, she had been challenged by someone who had attacked her psychically on many occasions. The attacks were part of a manipulation to control her with malicious intent. When this darkness finally came to the light, Joanna was able to deal with it effectively and make the attacks stop. During this underhanded battle against her, she kept herself in check to be sure she came from the power of compassion rather than the ego or sorcery.

Joanna shared with me after the regression that she had trained for many years with masters on how to invoke, identify, and dispatch dark-force entities - then replace them. Her training was specific and powerful, proving to be highly effective to deal with dark forces.

Her Soul Family explained that the experience immediately following her past life, where she was met by the High Priestess who represented the dark side, was Joanna's training to prepare her to battle even worse foes in her present life.

She knew just how to do it: she wouldn't permit her light to go to the dark. Joanna has had many experiences of this nature with her Collective Soul Family group.

I asked if this was part of her soul's life purpose? She said it was.

"I must destroy evil." Joanna explained that she has the gift of discernment to recognize the dark ones and to dispatch them.

During a conversation after her regression, I learned that Joanna was highly aware of the dark forces surfacing in the world at this time, such as extreme social injustices, government corruption, greed, and apathy. She was committed to saving the planet, dealing with the dark forces and bringing forth positive change. I learned that it has been her long term calling to dispatch evil so that the positive change can prevail.

She called herself "a soldier of the light." (I had chills!)

We discussed archangel Michael and how he is sometimes pictured as a mighty angel standing over evil with a double-edged sword stabbing a demon, much like she does.

This is where she has struggled with inner conflict. It's the part of her that has a deep concern about the rightness of doing this. This is the self-judgment she lives with.

In this present life, Joanna is supposed to awaken to the light and disavow the darkness. And this is what she has done even professionally for many years as an intuitive spiritual energy worker.

I asked for what purpose this served?

Joanna said, "For the ascension of human consciousness." She's on the front line and she's boots on the ground!

Her Soul Family is her shield, protection, and home, and they give her continual nourishment.

I asked if she was prepared for what she had to do here.

Joanna said this is the most critical time for her to come to her Soul Family and be with them for her personal safety. Since childhood, she has believed that she had to do this work all alone.

She already belongs to her Soul Family. She's an unbeatable force to the dark forces through their Collective. Without the Collective, the dis-unity will cause her to perish.

Now she realizes that, as long as she totally absorbs, realizes, and embraces her Soul Family as her shield, protector, and home, she can receive their rejuvenating and nourishing support. No longer alone, this was a game-changer for Joanna!

She also realized that if she tried to do it all alone, without them, she would perish before she was able to fulfill her goal of destroying the demonic reptilians and bringing in ascension consciousness on Earth.

Joanna's Soul Family showed her it's an error to think she must travel somewhere to be with her Soul Family. All she needs to do in order to be with her Soul Family is to go within. She's already a part of them.

They made a special point to tell her that they want her to communicate with them as much as possible, every day. Being with them will create a frequency where she'll be invisible to the dark force. It will be as though she has an invisible cloak, then "she can dispatch these reptoids!" They won't be able to trace her.

Coming back into harmony with her Soul Family, all threats move away.

She said that, while speaking to me, they used the word "we" instead of referring to her in second person as "she." They are one.

I asked if this was also archangel Michael's lineage?

Joanna said her Soul Family is like a wing of their shared lineage with archangel Michael. It's much like a royal blood line that goes straight through. "There are intermarriages that have their focus more towards healing as we all do."

There are also warrior healers because what is not whole is vulnerable to the dark. Dispatching the demons isn't enough. Love is at the core.

Whatever is non-love represents the forces of darkness. There's a point where compassion fails to assail dark forces and they go on and on and on. With archangel Michael, it's as though he's saying to the dark forces, "I'm casting you down to the pit where you belong!"

Her sweetheart of many years ago

We turned the subject to her male friend, the love of her life since a girl. I asked about him. Joanna told me that he had come to her when they were young. He was disguised to her as a simple man, not exciting. But his heart was beautiful! She remembered how immense his love for her had been. They were young when they loved each other, and even during previous lifetimes when they knew each other.

She explained that they haven't been able to be together in this life because she let her intellect, rather than her heart, make her decisions. However, this past year, she allowed her heart to open because the world had been opening its love to her. All her scaffolding and defenses were gone as she bravely allowed herself to feel her heartbreak with him from decades ago.

Shortly after this, she received a call from him. He told her that he had loved her all these years. Even though he was still married, he kept her pictures hidden away in a secret place. Hearing him speak, Joanna remembered the sweetness of his heart.

I asked why he was now in touch.

She said that the Collective wanted to tell her that the two of them will be talking in installments, learning who they are now.

During his magical call after so many years, and because she was so unguarded, she told him sweetly that he was the world's greatest kisser! We laughed. And then she opened up to him even more. Referring to her vulnerable, open self, he shared that he loves the feeling of who she is now. She surprised herself with what came out of her mouth on this call after he told her he loved her, when she said, "I love you too." She found herself with no reservation and it was unexpected and delightful for her to be able to be so open.

In that moment, she felt the world was reflecting back her open heart through the conversation with him. Joanna had a very sad and difficult childhood. She said that he was the one she trusted most in her entire life.

I asked if he was one of her Collective group?

She said that he isn't related by soul and wasn't of the same soul essence but that she had chosen a number of times to fall in love with him in past lives and they had shared hearts in less simple ways without being conscious of themselves as spiritual beings.

Joanna went on to tell me that they had been *travelers* in parallel lifetimes. They recognized each other from places they've been at the same time and became involved with each other. She shared that "traveler hearts and spirits" resonated with both of them. Even though they aren't soul mates, there's an eternal deep love between them that's hard to understand.

Do you two have spiritual work together?

It was explained that Joanna is for him as the Collective is for her. She is his "refuge." Staying open to him, present to him, she acts as his refuge. Learning this meant the world to Joanna.

What is he to Joanna?

"He's the only man I've ever loved and the person I gave my life to, then closed it." She no longer felt wary that they'd never be together. Nor did she feel wounded any longer. She described herself "in a space of delight." It felt like she was making up for what she couldn't give him when they were young and together.

To her, he is the emblem and sign that says, "All is healed," and she is able to love him unconditionally. The place of unconditional love proved a big opening for her.

Joanna went on to tell me that they can have a fruitful relationship now. Though he's thousands of miles away, she's his refuge. And he represents her ability to love unconditionally. They are both comfortable with each other today in this new way.

She felt so helped by learning that she is his refuge! And that he is her emblem for embracing her as unconditional love!

This allowed her to be enveloped in her Soul Family's love and to feel their strength and power.

Acting as an emissary for her Soul Family enables Joanna to embrace her own divine connection. "They are my ticket!"

I asked about her Soul Family and to describe their color and anything else she noticed.

Joanna said she saw outlines of their forms and they had a blue light around them. They were multitude in number. But there was a group of 8 or 9 in the forefront who had a *presence* and because of their unique oneness and energetic communications, they were also filters for the others.

This forefront group was her immediate family and the others were like an extended family. She realized that she was the 9th one!

They formed an open circle which opened and closed according to the energetics and focus they were engaged in - communicating through enfolding or counseling.

They were situated in rows like a small choir. The front row was her immediate Soul Family. They formed the semi-circle to hold her and to enfold her as their Collective energy spoke to her as one.

When they spoke of the dark places that she would be facing on Earth, the group closed their ranks around Joanna. They were protecting her. She noticed them as blue lights surrounding her so she could become invisible and this would protect her from dark forces.

It was a wonderful experience reuniting with her Soul Family and feeling inseparable from them. She explained that she could simply go within and they would be there.

How did her soul come into being?

Joanna explained that a soul is like a seed. There are many seed-like expressions that never blossom or take root. They depend on the environment and love to awaken the seed and to nurture it and provide what it needs in order to express itself.

She used the analogy of the acorn to the oak. The acorn isn't aware that it isn't already the oak. Its birth is mysterious to itself.

All souls begin as seeds of compact consciousness with inherent innate life force and specific individual expression. The motivating force is love.

Love exists on its own, infinitely and beyond. It is the force of all creation. If the acorn falls into a particular place, it can take life.

All things – stars, animals, beings – started out as seeds. Because of free will, many become distracted, where they get twisted and unable to grow straight and tall. Consciousness is so vast.

At this point, she announced that she had everything – and more – she needed from the regression. It was rich!

Following her regression, Joanna shared that the love she'd held for her sweetheart all her life had finally come to a place of peace. She was relieved. It had been a lifelong wound, now healed.

Joanna told me that she now realizes her need to always be united with her Soul Family for her refuge as well as her protection. She marveled that a year ago, she couldn't have done this kind of spiritual work but, since she opened her heart, it showed her how much more trusting she'd become.

Here's what I observed:

- I related to Joanna when she described herself as a spiritual healer and a soldier of the light. I was impressed with her confidence and knowledge in this realm.
- As a warrior against the dark, Joanna was also a brave warrior of the heart, allowing herself to feel the heartbreak from decades gone by. Her wounded feelings no longer pushed down, she was ready to learn how the unrequited relationship had changed and how to view it now.
- Some souls are travelers. In this way, they are able to have many broad experiences with great variety.
- I so loved the high purpose of her newfound relationship with the man she had loved for most of her life. He was now the emblem of her ability to love unconditionally. And she was his refuge! It was pure as angels.

During a regression, whenever there is a connection with the person's Spirit Guide, Master Guide, or Soul Family, I make a strong point to dwell there, interacting and asking questions. This helps my client to gain information and take it in at many levels for recall later.

My goal is to help my client make a strong connection with their guide. There is nothing more important and essential to our happiness and success than connecting with our group in Spirit World (or in Joanna's case, *ultra*-terrestrial Soul Family group).

In fact, I have found that the longer you can remain with your spiritual group or guide during a Spirit World Regression, the deeper the connection and more awakened you become. To me this is true enlightenment. As a regressionist, it's part of my work to help this occur whenever possible but it depends on my client's interest.

Our Spirit Guides want nothing more than for us to reconnect strongly and to remain in close touch at all times. In this way, they participate in untold ways to help, empower, guide, love, nurture, strengthen, and empower us. It's all they ask of us. And they wait and wait and wait for this connection to occur. Being in connection with our guides is the most powerful way we can live. The benefits are vast.

Imagine being like Joanna, suddenly arriving into human form for the first time and at a primitive period, being a brave pioneer soul – but without a clue as to what to do!

Joanna's regression revealed how far she'd come with her ability to trust, which was such a foundational thing to build her life on and it had been missing for so many years. She had felt alone and in despair all her life, just as she did in the past life. It had been her motif. Now she no longer felt alone. Her regression ran deep and could be life changing for her in many ways.

To recap: Joanna is a core essence of angelic "*ultra-terrestrials*" whose individual mission on Earth is to boldly deal with the darkness, much as archangel Michael is depicted doing. She does this by wielding her great light and, as a result, she brings in healing. In doing so, Joanna acts as a liaison to her Soul Family group and they act as one, participating in her incarnated experiences.

Until this regression, I had only heard of one other client who referred to themselves as "interstellar." Now, Joanna explained that it was bigger than "interplanetary" and far beyond planets. In fact, she called it inter-galactic and this is where her soul has traveled and incarnated.

I'm so happy when my clients make a strong connection with their Spirit World group, whether it's a guide, a Collective, or whatever it is that represents their spiritual group and home. If this meeting creates a strong and meaningful connection through the regression, my client will likely shift towards a life of connecting with them always. This changes their lives. And indeed, these regressions are transformational.

Each one of us exists in Spirit World at the same time that we live here on Earth. We leave a percent of our soul's energies at our soul home. There's tremendous power in uniting your Earth self with your Spirit self that represents who you truly are. Then divinity can truly come through us and be magnified on Earth. This is the way it works and what it means to have a spiritual life.

It's interesting how Joanna was prepared a year ago for her regression when she allowed for her heart to open. Only then could she have healing from her heartache, carried for all those years. It was the perfect setup for this regression. See how her Soul Family was at work to help bring this about? They know how to bless us.

I marveled at the beauty and high frequency of her and her long term friend's love for each other today. Rather than meeting at a level of personal need, longing, and attachment, they met on high spiritual ground, discovering each other as a refuge and emblem for unconditional love. How pure and revealing is the power of true love!

Joanna discovered that her path was not only to bring in ascension consciousness but also not to try and do it without connecting with her Soul Family or she would fail. This was a relief for her to no longer have to do it alone.

Chapter 12

Petrus

An Angelic Heart of Gold Confronts Ancient Oppression

Petrus and I knew each other a few years prior to being in contact about a regression. I held great admiration for him as a healer, author, and teacher. He was clearly all about love for humankind.

He had several questions to ask his Council of Elders.

One question was about his tendency to be self-critical. He wished to be able to really love himself unconditionally. A second question was about his immense difficulty meditating and he wanted to overcome it. He hoped a regression would reveal the ancient origin of these blocks. We also discussed his need to be healed of cancer or to know what was behind it.

Of the several past lives revealed, 3 stand out prominently.

Past life #1

The scene opened where Petrus found himself to be a high priest of ancient Egypt. He was in the Pharaoh's court. The year was about 1,000 B.C. and the two enjoyed a good relationship.

Petrus described his role and its great significance, which dramatically impacted the whole country.

It was believed by everyone in those days that the function of faith gave the type of spiritual care that could save them from all things, including poverty, hard times, and even the plague. It was also believed that the ceremonies were instituted by the gods and the minute observance and precision of them were essential for the survival of the country. He held the duty of performing rituals through ceremonies for the prosperity and well-being of all people. Petrus indicated that he deeply believed in what he did. So did the entire populace.

As he spoke, I felt his immense strength and commitment to duty, earnest devotion, desire to be of service, and pure holiness. He had been a spiritual man who held a position of enormous consequence for an entire nation.

I asked, "How does performing these ceremonies make you feel?"

Petrus explained that the ceremonies had to be performed carefully. There was an exactness required and there was a belief that he had to do the ceremonies "the right way." The country's prosperity depended on it. The ceremonies were performed out of duty, not love. Historically, love wasn't yet part of religious services.

I could sense the seriousness of his duty as high priest and the tension held in his role. Everything depended on him carrying out his duty perfectly.

Past life #2

In a second past life, we spent only a brief amount of time. His guide wanted to make a point similar to the previous past life.

Petrus lived in Geneva, Switzerland around the time of John Calvin, the great religious reformer. It was medieval times, perhaps the 16th century.

Everything was run in an extremely rigid manner including even what you could eat. Strict obedience to the many rules was required of everyone.

This caused enormous suffering for the people. The fear of hell played a major role in the belief that some people could suffer from a double pre-destination to hell! As Petrus described this, I felt his horror and disgust that this severe way of living affected everyone.

I noticed that in both past lives, Petrus spoke as being part of a Collective. His thoughtfulness towards others brought a great deal of care towards them. He lived in an unselfish way. This is true of his character in his present life as well and it tends to be the characteristic of a soul marked by a very high consciousness.

Past life #3

In a third past life, it was again medieval times, perhaps during the 11th century. Petrus was a peasant farmer living in a hut next to his lord's castle. It was a hard life fulfilling the demand of his lord, who took large portions of the yield of his farm. Even portions of his venison needed to feed his large family with 7 children had to be given to his lord.

The church was also demanding and there was rivalry between the lords and the church. Sometimes a lord took land from the church bishops. Other times the church excommunicated a lord for not obeying their rules.

Poor peasants were caught in their tug of war!

Petrus described his family as devout, scrupulous Christians who followed all that the church required, including giving up their goods. Once again, he was shown himself to be someone who was required to make great sacrifices and suffer hardship from being bound by strict rules, living under the burden of great oppression.

Although poor, he was happy and enjoyed great love for his family. He died at age 67, feeling very grateful, having successfully raised all 7 children, seeing them mature into adulthood.

Spirit World

Petrus died and as he floated away from his body, he said that he felt blocked in the regression. There was a feeling of oppression in his chest. And there was no guide.

Blocked

At that point, I regressed him more deeply so he could have a stronger access to Spirit World. As he took some deep breaths, I suggested that he simply allow himself to be free, letting go of doubts and anticipation about what was to come. I reminded him how much planning his guide had done to bring us together for the purpose for his regression and that they were very much with us at that moment. I also reminded him that it was not his responsibility to figure out Spirit World. It was the responsibility of his guide to show him.

Petrus said that the oppression he felt was as if someone was pressing down with both hands on his chest.

I asked, "If the feeling in your chest was represented by a color, what color would it be?" Petrus answered, "Gray brown." I asked, "And if we had a color that could sweep down into your chest and remove the gray brown, what color could would that be?" Petrus answered, "gold yellow." I told him that he could allow this to take place, as he let go and breathed into the gold yellow.

I counted to 3 and suggested that when I got to the number 3, the place that was gray brown, would then be replaced with gold yellow. And then he would be able to proceed with his regression with ease. I did this, reminding him that this was his moment of destiny with his soul and with his guide. The gold yellow would bring this about. This is what he deserved, and it was the moment for this to happen.

He felt a slight release in his chest, he said a 50% improvement. Once again, we discussed that in this very moment his Spirit Guide was helping him and enabling him to access his information and be free of the oppression. He was simply to allow this to happen.

I reminded him that he was in Spirit World, in the presence of his Spirit Guide, angels, and teachers. Whether or not he saw them, he could be open to their presence. As he opened up, he could allow the oppression to float away. It no longer belonged to him. We would allow his guide to remove this from his chest.

I felt we were actually in a potent healing moment where he was being released from the thousands of years being conditioned with oppression and rigidity, having to follow procedures exactly in order to have them work right. I felt this was the weight on his chest.

He reported that his chest was improving. As I spoke, I channeled healing for his great blockage of 3,000 years.

I told him emphatically that there was nothing on Earth that could stop him from being with his Guide. Nothing within him or within his history or his subconscious or his conditioning – past or present – which could prevent him from being with his Guide. As he was open to it, they would be causing the block to be removed and the opening to manifest for him.

As the high priest, he had been highly programmed to do things in a perfect way. The Calvin rigidity conditioned him, forcing him to follow the strictest rules. Certainly, as a peasant farmer under fiefdom, he had no freedom to determine things for himself due to strict oppression from his lord as well as the church.

But now, we were in an entirely different place under an entirely different time where we would allow his Spirit Guide to appear and interact. It was his spiritual right to have this occur.

I reflected, as I spoke to him, commenting on his character we'd been shown from his past lives. He was deeply devoted as a high priest and a Calvinist, as well as in the life as a peasant farmer. He not only followed the strict rules, but within him there was a concern for others, a desire to bless and an awareness of people suffering as well as a deep desire to have them alleviated from their hardships. His character was more powerful than and overrode the oppression he experienced.

I continued.

He's someone who cares deeply. In these past lives his love and compassion for others was clearly evident. He was heart centered even though he was forced to do things dutifully. I heard within his heart a love for principle, for good. And I saw this as an innate quality throughout his past lives as well as the present. I knew that I was viewing his angelic qualities.

I assured him that it was his soul's pure character which was leading him now and there was no longer rigidity or oppression. By this regression, we were enabling him to return to his soul of love and heart. This was all about freedom and liberation from the Dark Ages and ways which had carried over for so long! Now it could end.

It was time to break old vows and give himself permission to be free. Now he could actually drop the heavy burdens of his past and move into the light of his soul. It was time to be in his Higher Self which didn't require doing things in a perfect way. His Higher Self didn't require human rules or strictness or manipulation with fear in order to accomplish anything.

At this point, Petrus said that this was exactly what he needed to hear. He knew that this was his right and only the old voice would claim, "I'm not going to make it!" He had incarnated in the history of some of the most dark, rigid, difficult periods and he had chosen to enter these lives with his soul - a heart of gold.

As a poor, repressed, peasant farmer, he carried great gratitude in spite of his impoverishment. He also had love in his heart for his family. As a Calvinist, he had pure devotion. I felt his heart as the high priest of Egypt in wanting to do what was good for all. This is what drove him in each life. His Guide wanted him to know that they knew his goodness.

These lives were carried by love. Petrus was all about love. His love overrode everything. Today I felt his angelic presence because his love was so profound and pronounced.

His soul had elevated to what it is today at a master level, teacher of love. And now was time to let go of his entire past being bound by duty, rigidity, oppression, and forced to follow all the rules exactly. Now he had come to this life to be a man and a soul who had choice. In his present life, he had chosen a life of freedom and also of giving, compassion, healing, goodness, and teaching love. Love flows out of him.

In Spirit World, he's more like the same soul as he is on Earth. Today, before the regression, I wondered if he would notice a difference when he got to Spirit World, because he lives so close to who he actually is as his Higher Self. He is authentically spiritual.

Petrus follows light and love and makes deep sacrifices in order to do so. He is devoted to his soul's giving of his highest and best. He lives by the terms of his beautiful soul.

His chest was now fully free, without any feeling of oppression.

I told him that I felt the Council had been speaking to him through my voice. Nevertheless, I wished, once again, to ask for his Council to appear.

Just then, he sensed it was his absolute right that he have this breakthrough. I encouraged him to continue to release whatever he needed. I congratulated him for the excellent job he'd done throughout the regression in spite of strong doubts nagging at him, weighing him down with interference.

We'd seen the beauty of his aspiring soul and what it had been doing for thousands of years. We'd accomplished a lot! Now, we only wished to be with his Council and to be in a place of their guidance, healing, and love.

Just then, I was guided to change the subject. I asked, "What colors are your soul?"

He answered, "Deep blue, deep purple, and a little turquoise."

These beautiful colors represented him. I then asked, "What colors are mainly represented by your Council?" He answered, "Bright, bright, bright gold yellow." They represented a Collective, without a single spokesperson. They spoke as one.

The Golden Light was in front of him and at his sides. It was all-encompassing. As I spoke to Golden Light, I asked that they speak to me through Petrus's voice.

I asked Golden Light, "Is what I have been saying properly representative of why you brought Petrus to those particular past lives?" They answered, "yes."

I continued, "Is there something more we needed to understand regarding his past lives? Or are we complete now?" They answered, "Complete."

Continuing to press for more information, I asked Golden Light, "As a result of seeing these past lives so vividly, with Petrus's oppression and yet of his pure soul of love - the differences were like day and night - is that what you wanted Petrus to see today?" The answer was, "yes."

I questioned, "As a result of showing this to Petrus, is he now free of these past life vows and locked-in ways of doing things perfectly?" The answer came in, "much freer."

I asked, "How will Petrus have 100% freedom? Is this something which will happen mostly in this regression and then it will continue his healing later this evening? The answer was, "yes."

"Is the reason for which you brought Petrus to his regression today and the healing he needed, now complete?" Speaking for the Golden Light, Petrus answered, "yes."

I asked if his present life purpose was selected in order to express love. The answer was, "yes, expressing love – with his whole being."

I asked questions that represented other various things. Here's what we learned:
- He and his present wife have shared 11 past lives together.
- He is not primarily an Earth-based soul. He has incarnated on places other than Earth.
- He is of the Angelic Realm.

- He's incarnated on Earth 311 times.
- His angelic purpose is to be and express the soul of love, which is who he is.
- His wife is his soul mate and they share a global spirit of service in their present life. She is also of the Angelic Realm.
- He will be able to choose his moment of death in this present life. He is given full charge of this.
- When he passes on, in between his lives, his role is "bringing love".

I continued channeling Golden Light. Petrus's difficulty meditating was from the past lives shown to us in this regression. I shared with Golden Light that it felt Petrus had a real tightness about the meditative state, where he was bound by all the past life rules and rigidities which controlled and dominated him. We learned that this was true and it had been completely cleared now.

His continual concern that feels as though he has to "earn his salvation," had its roots from these past lives. Because we were informed that this work was 60% complete, we then asked Golden Light to please have him 100% released from all the fears of rules and rigidities and doing things in the right way - also to be free of the extreme necessity of doing ceremonies correctly and being bound by these practices.

(Note: I find that repeating healing treatment helps to have "the completion of a healing." Even though they said it was complete, I still review it another time or two in order to be thorough. This seems to work best.)

I knew Golden Light withheld nothing and that, as we continued to talk, this would allow Golden Light to fulfill his complete healing.

I acknowledged that this great moment of change in Petrus's life, which was occurring during this Spirit World Regression, which had covered thousands of years where he was basically chained, represented a moment where now, he could be without these obligations.

- I asked, "Is this also his physical healing of cancer? They didn't answer. I personally didn't think it was but I wanted to ask.
- I felt that the reason they brought Petrus to the regression was to release him from the oppression from the Dark Ages. This was his moment of freedom!
- As a result of being released, he will go into a "very high elevation." Golden Light answered, "yes," (to everything I was channeling.)
- They confirmed that this elevation would be a release from the belief of cancer. (That is exactly what had been coming to me intuitively, days before the regression.) Petrus confirmed that all of this made sense to him and was totally right, especially when I spoke to his real mission being "total love in all ways". It rang true inside his heart!

I shared with Petrus that the purple color is especially considered very high consciousness. I wanted to stay with the high elevation we were following, asking Golden Light for more insight.

I asked Golden Light, "Are you Petrus's guide while he's on Earth? The answer was, "yes, of course." (I had a strong feeling that whenever he leaves Earth, he is his own guide.)

I continued. "As he releases the rigidities and the extreme oppression, and as this freedom causes him to go into his soul's new elevated place, please tell us what his life will be like in this state of high elevation?" (It had already been established that at that point he would be released from cancer.)

"On a scale between 1-10, at what point is he now in the high elevation of his soul?" (10 being highest).

Golden Light answered, "glorious progress is possible. Very few people reach 10. It's not out of reach. He's in the sight of 10."

I asked, "Does Petrus have to die in order to be at a 10? Or can he do this while he's still here?" Golden Light answered, "He can do this while still present in his life."

Then Petrus added, "It will take greater dedication than before." As he added that sentence, I felt the energies of his past life and called him on it. We laughed. "Was that Golden Light? Or was that the ancient Petrus speaking?"

He agreed that it was the old voice and that it didn't sound like something that would come from Golden Light. I reminded him that doing things in the old way through hard work and extreme dedication and bound by duty were no longer part of him. It was the old self.

He integrated this into his soul as a result of the regression. His integration was still in process. I asked on a scale from 1-10, to what extent had he integrated his regression. He answered, "It only needed the flutter of a bird's wing to be a 10." I found this to be very poetic!

What came to me is, "This is about his freedom of soul and heart. This is his day of liberation and integration into his soul and his heart, allowing this to come into his life and be evident on Earth – no longer enslaved by his past." Even though his heart and soul are evident to all who know him in his present life, there is an even greater extent to which this is now occurring as a result of the regression. He agreed, "absolutely!"

I asked Petrus how he was feeling. He reported that:

- He felt lighter.
- He had the impression that the replies he gave for Golden Light were intuitively right. I shared that this is exactly how regression works, in an automatic way. It's called using your "active imagination." (You can read more about this in my book, *Past Life and Spirit World Regressions, Healing Through Revealing Soul*.)
- The breaking out of rigid rules was vitally important to him, seeing its origins of how he got stuck in these rules from his past lives. He's been on a conscious spiritual path historically for 1,000's of years.
- In some ways, it confirmed things he had thought intuitively were true about himself.
- Even though, before this regression he was clear that his life purpose was to express love, the regression confirmed this to him in a strong way. This felt important to him. He'll be much less concerned about meditation now because he doesn't have to meditate in order to be loving. As a result, he would "let that go."

I continued to channel. I spoke of him being integrated and elevated as a soul who is now liberated. The rules had been a great interference and his soul was shoving them out for good. Now, he will be able to allow his soul to be even more evident on Earth.

The confirmation of his healing of cancer was accomplished through the realization and revelation of the higher elevation of his soul. He can now let go of all the residue of past life energies and be free.

He had hoped that he could see and interact with his Council of Elders, and it was surprising this did not happen. However, his Council of Elders appeared as Golden Light, which is his Master Guide. I continued, "Golden Light is helping you through this present life but you are capable of being a soul that continues to evolve in high ways without anything more than your Higher Self." His consciousness is extremely evolved.

I spoke a little more about his soul, comparing him to a horse who'd been locked in a pen all his life. Then, one day, someone opened the gate and he was free to roam miles of green pasture and mountains beyond. He may stand there a moment to take it all in and what it meant. I felt that Petrus's soul was like a horse newly freed and can now begin to expand and roam the greater divine areas.

Releasing all impediments that had encumbered him before, he'd come back to his true self, his bigness, his inherent power, and he was safe to do so.

I explained that it's normal for his soul to expand, to feel free and liberated. It's his God-given right. A change had happened during the regression. Now it would be interesting to see how he proceeds in his life without ancient theological oppression. I felt he will come more into his soul-self and find the tremendous extent to which he is a soul at-large. There's a tremendous amount that awaits him.

The transformation felt great even though he was the same loving, caring, heart-based soul as always. The difference was that he now had freedom. He could let his wings open, much as a caterpillar that transforms into a butterfly, and he will soar. He now had permission to be who he needs to be as the angel that he is.

Petrus told me that what I said about his soul's new freedom had been "very, very important to him."

By his liberation, he'll be optimizing his spiritual power. The omnipotence that belongs to an angel will be his own. He won't have to bow to anything other than his own Higher Self, free as the angel that he is. He's the divine Self.

He will have the realization of his divine power by the authority of God to manifest healing and blessing. He can act by his own spiritual authority and power. In his conscious elevation, he will be able to make new decisions that come from his divine authority, to be who he needs to be as a liberated soul of love. He can achieve this with calm, quiet, peacefulness – and even be relaxed in doing so.

Here's what I observed:

- Even though Petrus used the intuitive skill of clairvoyance, viewing his past lives, I believe he had a stronger tendency towards Clair-cognizance, of simply *knowing* things that were true.

- He was expecting and hoping to have a visual experience and to be able to interact directly with his Council of Elders. Although this didn't happen, still the regression was totally successful. His Council turned out to be Golden Light, an iconic Master Guide, which is not represented as individuals who converse. Instead, Golden Light is a Collective divine presence of enormous, unimaginable spiritual power and love. In my experience from giving regressions where Golden Light appears, it tends to cause you to *know* things. I believe this is how it was supposed to be for Petrus.
- In the beginning of our session, relaxing into a regressed state was difficult for Petrus. His mind was active, interrupted by strong, insistent, doubtful thoughts making him believe the process wasn't working and that he couldn't do it. He had a lot of blocks. Such oppression he was under! Slowly, we were led through the blocks as I let the Angelic Realm guide me.
- I recalled the oppression he felt on his chest and the gray brown that represented it. He said that he needed the color yellow gold in order to clear it. It was much later in the regression that we learned that his Spirit Guide was Golden Light. This is was what healed him. His intuition was deeply connected when he *knew* his chest needed yellow gold to help him.
- You may notice that the latter part of our session was highly, extraordinarily celestial. It impressed me that he was able, after several hours of a session, to be able to have the energy and spiritual stamina to reach for these high

levels. He told me he was full of energy in his 80's!
- I can go far and wide in my soul readings, but most people are satisfied and filled before I can reach the full extent of my insights on soul. This regression with Petrus was personally fulfilling to me because, not only did he allow me to go on and on, it was as though we two were matched in desire to see more of the infinite! I felt we reached an all-time height of spiritual vision together. We shared God-moments of utter spiritual bliss. I was so delighted to know his authentic self, his beautiful soul of love, love, love!

Chapter 13

My Own First Regression Meeting Mother Mary

I've personally had about 56 regressions.

Each one has given me deep insight into myself as a soul and they have, overall, dramatically changed my life because of a deeper understanding of my true self.

The following was my first Spirit World Regression. I hardly slept the night before this, so excited to see what I would learn. There is nothing that would have prepared me for what I was about to discover!

Past Life

It was 1846 and I liked my life. My name was Mary. Enjoying a village life, I lived in Ireland near the seaside. I was all about family and home, and I felt happy and loved. Following this brief insight, I was ready to move forward. I immediately went to Spirit World. There was no death experience.

Spirit World

I became aware of an immensely loving presence which appeared as a beautiful being of light with a special color of blue at the heart and a center of golden light radiating outward. I realized that she knew me. Her name was Mother Mary and I was instantly overwhelmed by her magnificence and her knowledge of me.

Tears streamed down my face as I took in her spiritual grandness. I described her as a white light extending 23,000 miles in length. Her blue was a "perfect blue." I've never witnessed such a presence!

When she began speaking to me, her voice sounded like music that filled everything. This magnificent being became a heart that spoke pure love. As she poured out her love on me, I was filled with calm and beauty. It seemed that I knew her to be myself, although I didn't understand what this meant. It made no sense to me.

I heard an inner voice, "I've been her for a long time." I was confused. My regressionist gently asked me not to analyze it, advising me to just stay with the unfolding moments within the regression.

As I continued, I felt calm and known by her. I noticed that her voice sounded like a low tone flute. It was beautiful and serene. Mary's presence filled me and gave me great comfort.

Mother Mary spoke directly to me

Mary spoke to me and said, "Shannon is Mother Love. She's been fully initiated, and she knows it. I trust her. She truly is Mother Love." Then she added, "She has the blue."

The regressionist asked me to imagine a full body mirror in front of me, look at the reflection, and describe what I saw. I described it to the regressionist:

"My essence and appearance are exactly like Mother Mary. (I remember thinking, 'But how can that be?')

I'm shaped in a long, slender line. The top of my head is outlined in a dome shape. There's a robe trailing, going down my back about 23,000 miles long. It's made of white light.

I'm very simple. I'm all about love. Some of my love gifts are comfort, assurance, peace, healing, caring, and joy. These emanate to others. My love is powerful and can perform anything. Nothing is impossible. Everything is possible. I carry the possibility of everything – including healing. This is my spiritual energy. It's also all around me."

Mary informed me about my present life

She told me that she taught me about family and how it works along with understanding the mother's importance. The mother carries Mary's harmony in everything, including the household food, her hugs and smiles, and when she holds someone's hand. The mother's harmony is one of Mary's functions. She told me I've been given the gift of beautiful families over many lifetimes and she said, "You're very good at this."

Mary introduced me to her trainees

Five small, white lights appeared and wanted to speak to me. They were situated in a straight line, next to each other. I noticed they had the same dome shape outline at the top of their heads. They seemed to be connected together by their white lights. I called them "domes of light."

It was explained to me that the white lights and myself were all emanating Mother Love. However, I didn't notice any blue color in them. Mary told me that they knew who they were as Mother Love, just like me.

She said, "These are my trainees. Shannon is there too, but she has the intense, vibrant royal blue light. Her soul is more mature. The white lights are going to eventually become blue as they go along. They're training to be Mother Mary.

This is the mission. We need Mother Love on Earth to spread her wings of love and be magnificent as a powerful presence – to be felt, known, and loved, so that everyone will feel her embrace and know her.

As a result of this, a giant transformation will take place. It will be huge, affecting the entire universe.

Shannon was brought in as an example of what another Mary looks like and what she can do."

She went on to explain that the next level of the trainees' mission is that they would be sent out to learn and practice Mother Love. She would be with them. They would be training on Earth to grow and develop who they are so they could become who they were meant to be – Mother Love. Mary explained that this was for the purpose of making a major imprint.

Mother Mary's personal instructions to me

Mary told me I needed to use my blue to drape over Earth because Earth needed it. She informed me that I knew about my blue and that this is the right time to use it.

I spoke about what I began experiencing.

"I'm penetrating Earth with the blue. It's going all the way through Earth. I can see it happening. Earth has the blue now. I pour my love into Earth. When I cover Earth, I'm in my right place. My blue penetrates with love, healing, and transformation, offering immense help to others.

The blue heals suffering. It goes to those crying, in trouble. (I was crying, so touched by this experience).

My blue is an immersion for all. I've done this for a longtime, but I need to do it larger scale now. I must remember to keep covering with my blue. Allow it to permeate wherever there's hurt, pain, and suffering. Besides humans, my blue also goes to alleviate suffering with animals, plants, trees, air, and water. I'm covering all of Earth and carrying love everywhere now. It's vital that everyone receives my blue. This is my responsibility and I must not let up. I'm committed. I didn't know I was supposed to do it but I'm created big so that I can do it."

I had a sense that I've been doing this for Earth for over 100,000 lifetimes.

Council of Elders

I was taken to visit my 5 membered Council of Elders. They were sitting at a semi-circular shape table. The walls behind them were alive. The Council members had the dome-shape outline just like mine and Mary's. The middle Elder was the spokesperson.

I noticed how huge I was, cosmic sized, in fact. My Council was much smaller. They told me I had to be huge in order to cover Earth and the love intention that I carried in my heart had to be huge. It was a necessity.

The middle Elder was male and wore a crown of light, which was jewel toned.

They were on a platform but because of my vast size I had to float and was mostly towering above and directly in front of them.

I thought of us as the "blue domed beings." They were about to address me.

The mission

The Council shared that they brought me to them in order to discuss the present timing which coincided with my life's mission. They communicated telepathically and they spoke as one. They explained that the need was great and that I had been prepared. They said that I knew how to go into action and that, even though I had not consciously known about my powerful blue until now, I can exude it easily and could meet important needs.

They told me that I'd been sending out my blue light of love in this present life since I was a child, when I helped my mom assist the County Welfare Department's foster home babies to take them for their vaccine shots. I recalled those car rides, where mom and I poured our love and affection over these precious babies. We bonded with them and they had our full attention and love during those times.

The Council reminded me how I responded to my heart's longing for the babies not to suffer and for them to be placed with good mothers and fathers soon. I didn't realize that I had been engaged in my life mission even then.

They instructed me how to give my blue to Earth and they told me this would give enormous relief and comfort – reducing a great deal of suffering.

"Start at the top of Earth and begin draping it with your blue. As the blue descends, it saturates everything. You can do it."

Mary told me, "This mission is even bigger than Earth. It's universal, the ultimate experience of love!"

Each Elder addressed me

The spokesperson told me I was being initiated and this was my moment to come into the realization of this destined moment when I would go into action. (I was, of course, captivated but also felt overwhelmed with disbelief.)

Elder #5 was on my right. He infused me with the gift of power. I knew this power and felt its limitlessness instantly. This power entered through my heart and expanded into my blue so it could go into bold action immersing all of Earth. For some strange reason, this all made sense.

As this occurred, I saw a large map of Earth. The blue was going into continents where people needed care – to places that children were working as slaves, to refugee camps hosting masses without homes and experiencing great duress, to women who were being abused, and to men crying in despair. Many instances of both large scale and individualized suffering flashed before me. I often carry similar images of suffering in my heart, where I'm suddenly aware of terrible sufferings on Earth and I pray.

It was explained to me that the blue color was creating new patterns and structures on Earth to hold love. The blue was doing the work. I was told that there was a willingness and cooperation on Earth now because there is a deep sense that this is what is most needed and will work. It was explained to me that resistance would go away and dissolve into a willingness and openness. I thought to myself, "It's a good thing I'm big!" (I felt like an ant being told to go out and help the world.)

Other gifts given to me by my Council

In addition to Elder #5's gift of power, I was also given additional gifts.

Elder #3 wore a captain's hat and I learned that he's captain of the Mother Ship of Love. He has maps where he navigates and reveals openings to me, assuring me that I'll find my way into these important openings and that I won't get stuck. Once again, I was told there will be little resistance to love. He'd be working with me sharing his maps and important openings.

Elder #2 was an expander who told me I could be as big as I needed. He will help me expand my love in unbelievable ways. He said, "Universal expander, no problem!"

Elder #4 gave me the gift of remembrance so that my life carries the remembrance of love within every breath of my body – in my heart, mind, soul, cells, tissues, and fiber. I will receive full support for remembering the blue and the love needed and my part in it.

The Council of Elders advised me to not get dismayed. "Quit looking at the dark and keep bringing in the light, pouring the love." I recognized this as my job. They assured me that I would grow in this work and there would be more love as a result. "Love is all that we need."

They asked me to call on them – Mother Mary and my Council of Elders. They are always with me and whenever I call on them, the right one would come forward and respond. Collectively they said, "We are the Council of Love and we are Masters of Love." (I had chills. My husband, Scotty, and I often talked about our "High Council," without having evidence of one but we often felt this as a presence with us in our work to spread the understanding of love. And we taught classes on love mastery.)

They said there was an urgency for my work and, if I'll take care of flooding the planet and everyone and everything with love, they will fix the rest. Everyone has to have love. Love is like the water that comes to the dry desert to bring new life. Earth needs to be flooded with the water of love. It will be an immersion of love. I'll grow and learn more as I go. And as I do the flooding, it will teach me, and many new insights will come. I'll get better through my practice of flooding with love. It will change everything. I will go first to do this, using my blue. Then, Scotty will have a teaching role. And many will follow.

As we completed, I was aware of feeling love coursing through me like a powerful energy of a waterfall. It was profuse. I was fully immersed in love. It was everywhere. It was very familiar to me.

Mother Love said, "And then they will know me."

Here's what I observed:

- From the moment I met Mary, my endless curiosity about her took over my entire life. For this reason, I decided to become trained as a regression counselor and enlist my dear husband to join me so that together we could explore this vast realm of soul, offering each other many regressions. Together we have had over 100 regressions. We would never be the same. These regression experiences have shaped who we have become today.
- Since this first regression, I have become far more sensitive to suffering, touched by greater empathy and often felt overwhelming love and deep compassion. I've grown in love and tenderness.
- I've thought a lot about the blue referred to in my regression. I've come to understand intuitively that the blue is synonymous with love and it represents a very high and powerful vibration that heals. I'm familiar with this energy. I often feel it coursing through me as though I am being flooded with it. It's powerful. It's the love that poured through my book, *Love Heals, How to Heal Everything with Love*. During the regression, I had a visual of my blue love covering Earth in the shape of angelic wings. It felt both intimate and affectionate to cover and hold Earth in such enormous love.
- In early 2000, my husband and I co-founded a virtual website called *The Love Center* (www.thelovecenter.com). We made over 100 short videos teaching how to become a Love

Master. It was based on 60 love skills from our book, *The Top 60 Love Skills You Were Never Taught, Secrets of a Love Master*. Now many years later, it is interesting that I would meet with my Council of Love who are Love Masters! They surely had been our guides. It's fascinating that both Scotty and I had the same vision of how to teach love through our workshops, books, and virtual courses. This is what happens when you're partnering with your soul mate on your soul mate journey together. This passion to have love known, felt, and understood, has driven our lives.

- We've been on a long-term path of writing other love books including, *The Love You Deserve, A Spiritual Guide to Genuine Love* and also *Soul Mate Love, Inside Secrets of an Authentic Soul Mate Couple*. This has been our life purpose, to teach and spread love on Earth. We've had, what seems like, a million conversations about love and we've written thousands of pages on the subject. So many people are confused by love and experience hurt, not love, in their most intimate relationships. There's vast ignorance about love. Love has been mistaken for an emotion and sorely missed within relationships. It's time to reclaim love and its power. True love is a divine force that created you and it lives within you waiting to be discovered and utilized. It carries many principles and requires much of us to enact in our relationships to each other and to the world. The universe is powered by love. This love must now enter our relationships.

- In a number of my many subsequent regressions, I was shown a vision of what's to come. It revealed a new Earth and culture, one filled with sweetness, kindness, unity, caring, and heart-felt love. The vision revealed that far more joy and love will characterize families, friends, and communities everywhere. These relationships will be the center of our lives and even form our companies, organizations, and governments. I believe that we are on course for this to occur. There will come an astounding change that will be life altering for us all. My Council of Love said that it was going to be successful. Everyone will be involved.
- Being my first regression, I realized that it addressed the two questions that I've wondered about since a child. "Who am I?" And, "What is my purpose?" Discovering answers to these two questions has guided my life and its value.
- During my regression, when I first saw Mary and the dome shaped outline of her head, I instantly recalled seeing this same dome shape outline on Michelangelo's Mary in his masterpiece *The Pieta*. When I first viewed this magnificent statue in the Vatican City, I stared a long time at her dome shape head as I took in the pitiful, heart-breaking suffering this stunning statue depicted of Mary holding the slain Jesus in her arms. Mary was huge.
- When I first met Mother Mary during the regression, in the back of my mind, I wondered what Mary this was. Was it Jesus's mother? Who was this Mary? As I have grown in understanding over the years, Mother Mary, I

believe, is the powerful Master Guide of the Angelic Realm and she is truly divine, universal, infinite Love – including its source and everything encompassing it.
- One day, years before this regression, I felt compelled to use colored pictures and draw my soul's self-portrait. Oddly, I drew myself as a blue color (a specific blue shade) that was draping itself over Earth. It felt like my blue was pure love. In the picture, my drape covered about 1/3 of Earth and it would continue to drape itself over it entirely. Earth was situated among the universe's stars. I then drew Scotty's soul as the color yellow-gold that was like a universal grid, a Golden Light, covering and uniting everything, everywhere. It was amazing to me that I was experiencing confirmation about this during my regression.
- For a long while after this startling regression, I carried great doubts about myself and questioned, "Who am I, little me, to believe I carry a role of such importance?" I'm conditioned, like most, to believe that important roles of saving Earth are headed up by giant non-profit institutions and their massive contributors and devoted genius leaders and tireless volunteers. It took a long time for me to come to terms with this information about myself as Mary. I've contemplated it for years since the regression and I've come to a greater understanding. One thing I have learned is that:
  - what appears as my important role on Earth, represents a microcosm of each of us in our divine, infinite importance. Most

of us don't give a fraction of credit to our absolute essentiality in life – its power to contribute vastly to the whole. This is an invitation for you to step outside your "little" self and expand into your soul and its great worth.
  - it is the power of love and its principles that uphold all life. (*Power vs. Force* by Dr David R. Hawkins.) Whenever you adhere to basic principles of love, it is carried in your energy field. Divine Principles generate attractor energy fields which can become "M fields." These are the generators which determine true power and are the origin of spiritual transformation on Earth when adhered to.
- Another insight I gained since the regression is that I believe I'm a representative of a Collective which represents Mary. This Collective includes Mary, my Council of Love Masters, the 5 dome lights in training, and myself. Although I may be the only one who is presently on Earth, all of these heavenly hosts are with me and we are acting as one.
- Since Scotty and I met 28 years ago, our life purpose has been the subject that has been most discussed in our marriage and which has driven our life decisions. One of our first books, *Liberating Your Magnificence, 25 Keys to Loving and Healing Yourself*, shares some of the ways used to help us discover our life purpose. I've come to understand that it is the principles that you live by – compassion, justice, fairness, joy,

love, peacemaking, caring, generosity, tenacity, devotion, commitment, honesty, empathy, and such – which cause you to carry power and value in your life. The playing field is level for us all. Anyone can enter this field and practice the mastery of love's principles, which transform you as well as influence those around you for the better. This is what I believe. You don't have to be seen, known, celebrated, or perfect. Just be your best self and you will achieve your highest life purpose. This is the path of each soul. You carry greatness within you.

- As a result of Spirit World Regressions, I am stronger in knowledge of my Higher Self and I am more aware of making choices that align with my soul. Like us all, I have a very far way to go. But the way is lit for us by the love of our Spirit Guides, Master Guides, Council of Elders, Archangels and the Angelic Realm, and our Soul Families. It means a great deal to me that I am not alone doing my mission. Neither are you. We travel this path together, forever, and we need each other to succeed, to love each other through it all. Together, we will make love the living reality that it is meant to be on Earth – in our hearts, minds, bodies, and lives as well as for our beloved planet and universe.

About the Author

Shannon Peck is a certified Past Life Regression and Spirit World Regression counselor. She utilizes Past Life and Spirit World Regression as a powerful tool to help clients discover their identity as a soul, their life purpose, and to find healing.

As an interfaith minister, she has been a spiritual healer for over 30 years. Known as a "Love Healer," her work is centered on the healing power of divine Love.

She is also a certified Usui Holy Fire III Karuna Reiki Master Teacher and often utilizes Reiki healing energy during regression sessions.

Shannon has a global practice spanning U.S., U.K., Canada, France, Greece, Italy, Australia, Mexico, and Japan. She lives in sunny San Diego with her soul mate husband, Scotty.

For lots of love and healing, visit

www.ShannonPeck.com

Contact or Book a Session with Shannon

I'd love to hear from you! To contact me with questions or to book a regression – in person or by Zoom - you can reach me at:

ShannonPeck@gmail.com

A free gift and more information is waiting for you at:

www.ShannonPeck.com

I look forward to hearing from you.

Love,

Shannon